WORTH the WAHALA

"NOTHING WORTH HAVING COMES EASY"

BORLEY G QUAYE

Worth The Wahala

Copyright © 2017 by Borley Quaye

All rights reserved.

Cover credit: RvreCreator
Back cover credit: The Tri60 Group

ISBN-10: 0-9988987-0-8
ISBN-13: 978-0-9988987-0-4

Heyborley.com
Email: borleyquaye@gmail.com

Contents

Worth the Wahala

Nothing Worth Having Comes Easy

CHAPTER 1

WORTH THE WAHALA?

I love the word Wahala. Let me use it in a few scenarios so you can learn to love it too.

Imagine that you've planned to go to the weddings of two of your closest friends this month, but later find out that your boss wants you to work overtime on those days. You get so upset and complain, "My work schedule causes way too much Wahala in my life!"

Okay, that was fun. But let's switch it up.

Your old boo is in town out of the blue and he wants to see you. You have barely agreed to go out with him and he's already asking you to pick a restaurant and make all the arrangements. You are tired from work, have nothing to wear, and just started a new diet. So, you text him, "You know what? I'd rather not go through the Wahala. I'll just sit at home, watch The Mindy Project, and eat one of my paleo meal preps." How rude of you, but I love it!

You see? The word Wahala is the bomb.com.

Wahala is drama.

If you ask my dad what the word means, he'll simply say 'trouble'.

A guy I used to date used Wahala to describe the 'trouble' he thought I was putting him through. Throughout our little friendship, he kept trying to get me to partake in sinful activities but I would always say no. During one of our usual arguments about why I wouldn't send him a picture of this or agree to that, he simply asked, "why do you put me through so much

Wahala?!"

The answer to that question is quite simple. Because I'm worth the Wahala.

That dude was not my husband, not my boyfriend, and barely even a boo. He was nothing to me. When I looked down at my ring finger and the-canary-yellow-pear-cut-diamond-engagement-ring-blinging-so-much-that-I-had-to-squint, was still imaginary. I knew he didn't deserve a nude pic, intimacy, or whatever else he was begging me for? He thought he deserved these things but he failed to recognize my true value.

I am worth dying for.

I am the child of a King. I am royalty. Despite my many flaws, I am famous in my Father's eyes. I am special to someone. I am worth opening doors for. I am worth the call and not just the text. I am worth patience and kindness. I am worth a little outside-the-box thinking. I am worth going above and beyond for. Yes, I am worth the Wahala. And trust me, there is going to be some Wahala.

I am not suggesting that we act crazy and expect everyone to deal with it. That's not the Wahala we are discussing here. We are discussing the inconveniences experienced while making the decisions to do what is right in your life. My old boo felt inconvenienced when I told him I wasn't having sex until marriage, but I'm worth the Wahala. I feel inconvenienced when I have to interrupt my busy schedule for a gym session, but I'm worth the Wahala. I know exactly who I am and I know my worth. I know the skills that I bring to the table. I know the loyalty and love I have within me to give to my relationships, to my career, and to my passions. I know my weaknesses and that I'm worth the time it takes to better myself. I am worth the Wahala. I want you to able to say those words with absolute confidence by the time you finish reading this book.

Throughout this book, I want to encourage you, especially the young women, to be secure in your values and moral foundation. At the same time, I want to give you a practical guide to living the right way in a crazy world. Being morally secure will allow you to distinguish between right and wrong, but living a moral life requires bold decision-making because society says doing the right thing is whack. I like to use examples involving romantic relationships to illustrate many of my points (because a lot of issues young woman have stem from relationships and men), but please note that the principles can be applied to many other areas, such as work and family relationships.

At the end of each chapter, you will find a list of the scriptures referenced or quoted within that chapter. You don't have to be Christian to read this book. I want to encourage everyone to be open to accepting these concepts and not turn away from this book because of the scriptures embedded within these pages. Read them and decide if they make sense for your life. There is also a section in the back of the book where you can record scriptures and make notes about points that stick out to you. Use these resources! When you are finished, pass this book on to a friend!

One more thing! Over the next several chapters, I might refer to you all as chale. In Ghana, chale means friend. It is kind of pronounced like Charley but said really fast and in a West African accent. Now, since we are all friends and are worth the Wahala, let's jump right in!

CHAPTER 2

THE ROOT OF YOUR WORTH

We are heirs of the Most High King. Let that sink in.

You are a descendant of the King of Kings–the One who created the heavens and the earth. There is nobody like Him. He was and will always be the Man with the plan. He is the One who is always steps ahead of the rest. He is revered, respected, and all-powerful.

Your earthly father may be far from a king, but our spiritual Father is the bomb.com. He literally is everything. If that doesn't give you warrant to walk around with your head held high, then I do not know what will.

You know those people who walk around like their 'you know what' doesn't stink? I'm talking about the blonde from Mean Girls, Hillary from The Fresh Prince of Bel-Air, and Scar from Lion King. Or Scott Disick from Keeping Up with the Kardashians who calls himself "Lord Disick" and, on one episode, actually shoved a hundred-dollar bill down his waiter's mouth.

Why do these people have such an elitist attitude and pretentious demeanor? Because they have confidence. Whether it comes from security due to family legacy, their future prospects, or their bomb jollof making skills, they have something that gives them pride. Minus the overbearing pretentiousness, this is the confidence I want you to have.

Do not be confused! I'm a firm believer in humility. I think that you should greet the janitor with the same respect as you would greet the CEO. However, I want you to have pride in who you are and what you have. You are royalty. You have access to the most powerful God in creation and He thinks that you are pretty freaking amazing. P.S. This does not give you permission to shove a hundred-dollar bill in a person's mouth.

Ok, it's activity time! Find a mirror and look at yourself (your iPhone selfie-screen works too). What do you see? If you are anything like me, you just got off work and look a hot mess. When I look in the mirror, I see frizzy hair, cheeks that are a little too chunky, and a huge zit that decided to pop up out of nowhere on this day of all days—the day I decide to describe my current self to the readers of my first book.

God created you just the way you are—both the good parts and the bad—and loves everything about you. He loves your style and what you decided to throw on today (even if your little sister thinks that you look an absolute hot mess). He loves the way that your eyebrows grow in when you are a few days past your threading appointment. Interestingly enough, God wants you to appreciate yourself, flaws and all. I am learning to love the way that I swallow down full meals in less than 3 minutes. Okay, I'm not going to lie. I don't exactly love that I overeat, but I love that He made that one of my 'things to work on'.

Imagine, the CEO of the best and largest business in the world has created, molded, and hired you to be His lovely employee and to do a job for Him. And because He's such a great boss and is so successful, He is even willing to work one-on-one with you to make you the best person that you can possibly become. God wants the best for us and for us to know our worth. He doesn't want us to associate with people who don't deserve to employ us. (I mean we do have a pretty impressive resume!)

He wants us to take what we've learned from Him and help other people who want to have the same job, skills, and happiness that we have received. Ephesians 2:10 says "For we are God's handiwork, created in Christ Jesus to do good works, which God prepared in advance for us to do." This powerful passage shows us, not only does God love us just the way we are, but that He also wants us to fulfill a unique task for Him and to do good deeds.

Okoto nwo anoma is a Ghanaian proverb that means a crab does not give birth to a bird. If we were birthed from the image of God, how can we be anything but royalty?

When I was sixteen, my grandmother gave tiaras to each of her granddaughters, myself included. She told us that they were not to be worn at all times, but rather to serve as a symbolic reminder that we are daughters of the Lord. She wanted us to remember that we are royalty and that we should carry ourselves with dignity. This year, on my 27th birthday, I received my first text from her ever (yes it is 2017. She's a little late!). It read:

Happy B'Day Borley! Remember your crown.
Love Grandma <3

A crab does not give birth to a bird.

Chale, know your worth and take pride in yourself. Remember your crown. You are worth the Wahala.

Scriptures referenced:

2 Corinthians 12: 9 - And He has said to me, "My grace is sufficient for you, for power is perfected in weakness." Most gladly, therefore, I will rather boast about my weaknesses, so that the power of Christ may dwell in me. (NASB)

Ephesians 2:10 - "For we are God's handiwork, created in Christ Jesus to do good works, which God prepared in advance for us to do." (NIV)

Chapter 3

OUT WITH THE OLD & IN WITH THE NEW

2014 was a year of intentional singleness for me. Prior to that year, I had a bad habit of keeping guys around just to fill time and space. Guys who really didn't share my values. So I decided to truly focus on myself, not because I was heartbroken and needed to regain strength or anything, but to concentrate on my own self-improvement and discover who I was without 'boy-fog' clouding my decision-making.

Boy-fog is real. For example, you might think you want that jerk who takes you out to dinner all the time but maybe you really just like going out to eat. You may actually be lonely or may simply enjoy going out, but now boy-fog is confusing you into thinking that you like a guy because of what you do together, rather than because of who he is.

I decided to be intentionally single because I wanted to walk into a room and not worry about what the guys around me were thinking, but to instead focus on the true purpose of the gathering. I wanted to focus on making genuine friendships and get to know men without thinking about how to get them to like me. I needed space from the drama and time for Borley. I wanted to excel in my job, get a grasp on my budget and finances, start new projects, and write a book! I wanted to learn, to live, and to see life through a new lens. Most importantly, I wanted to focus on living my life for Christ.

We have to find out what we really want out of life. My 'time-off' from dating allowed me to refocus on my values and my goals so that when the time came for me to date again, I wouldn't settle. See, focusing on what you want doesn't only apply to dating preferences. It includes seemingly simple choices such as what to eat as well as more difficult decisions such as career choices.

During my year of intentional singleness and self-focus, I realized that if I didn't want do something, I didn't have to do it.. You might be thinking, 'well Borley, I never do anything I don't want to do.' Good for you, but I used to all the time. I've bought an expensive purse before just because my sister said "Just do it. It's not like you don't have a job." Also, while visiting London for the very first time, I followed the crowd to a boring French restaurant when I was really dying to try English fish and chips. I have gone to countless clubs and parties with friends—knowing that it's not my scene—simply because I didn't want to be the oddball out. I stopped doing things I did not want to do. However in 2014 I really learned to put my needs and myself first.

I started eating the cheap and delicious street food that I wanted and I also splurged on the healthy airport food that I knew would make me feel good after a long trip. I didn't stay up later than I wanted, nor did I feel bad about inviting my friends over for dinner and a movie when I had expended my restaurant budget for the month. I returned that purse my sister told me to buy after it sat on the top shelf of my closet for almost a month.

The first step to living a life of value is figuring out what you want. Write down what you want out of life. What do you want to accomplish in the next five years? What do you want your husband to be like? Where do you want to live? What do you want to do in your free time? What do you want to do to earn a living? I'm about to say something really crazy:

Figure out the life you want to live and *start living it*.
Be specific. If you want to be in a relationship, simply saying you want a relationship is not enough. You have to describe

the kind of relationship you want to be in. On the other hand, if you are in a bad relationship that you want to leave, you need to realize that your life is tick-tocking away and you're not doing anything to change your situation. That has to end now!

Yikes, easier said than done, right? Getting out of any-thing—whether it is a job, relationship, housing, whatever—is not easy. Now, I'm not saying that you should turn in your two-week resignation and call off your engagement, but you should make feasible plans towards living the life you want, and then actually live that life. You can do it. You want to quit eating meat? Do it. Your friends will not die because you can't do dinners at Fogo de Chão anymore. It's hard to get up one day and say, "enough is enough, I'm done,"—but you can. **Your task, first and foremost, is to write out what you want.**

Take a pen and paper and make a list of what you think you deserve. If you feel comfortable, write it in the notes sec-tion in the back of this book. When you're done, look over your list and edit it, add to it, and embrace it—daily. You can read over what you want and compare it to what you have. I have a yearly vision board that I refer to and another one that is a five-year vision board! They are constant reminders of what I want and what I need to work towards.

If you haven't already made one, gather a group of your girlfriends and have a vision board party! It actually takes a lot longer than you would think, but it's fun! Grab some maga-zines, glue, and gluten-free pizza to make it a night. Guess what? You deserve it!

Let me take a step back and tell you a little bit about my-self so you will understand where I'm coming from in the fol-lowing pages.

I am a sweet Georgia Peach mixed with some South Caroli-na, G.R.I.T.S (girls raised in the south—Sorry G.R.I.T.S. I couldn't keep the secret to myself.). I spent the first 12 years of my life in Stone Mountain, a suburb of Atlanta. Then I moved to Hartsville, South Carolina for middle school and high school before I moved back to ATL for college at the one and only Spelman College. I went from a city private school, to a rural public school, and back.

I was raised by a stern, Ghanaian father and a free-spirited, White-American mother. They are also both medical doctors. I wasn't allowed to wear two-piece bathing suits until I was a teenager, and even then I had to be subtle about it so my dad didn't change his mind. I am the middle child of five very different siblings. When I was younger, I would climb into my older brother's crib to make him cry and orchestrate 'children living room theatre' to entertain the family at holiday gatherings.

I appreciate my West African upbringing, which strongly imparts the importance of respect. I appreciate the spiritual and educational foundation from my Christian preschool and elementary school where I spent most of my days and nights for the first decade of my life. I appreciate what the 'Killaville' streets of Hartsville taught me as a teenager. I appreciate Spelman College for bringing it all full circle, painting a vivid picture of what society would be like for me and how I could tackle it with class. From these experiences, I am able to write this book.

When I told my dad I no longer wanted to become a doctor, he didn't talk to me for four straight months. Chale, I would walk into a room, try to speak to him, and he wouldn't even acknowledge my presence. Until that point, I had worked so hard in college to do what I had to do to become a doctor (good grades, internships, research, etc), but I was never the smartest peach in the plum tree. Now, don't get me wrong, I wasn't an idiot, but it was just really hard for me to stay afloat in my pre-med courses. This was also probably due to the fact that I was working towards something that I only had minimal

15

interest in.

But I kept at it because I felt so much pressure to make my dad proud of me because he had invested so much time and money into my future. He told me that his last life goal is to make sure that one of his kids got into medical school. (Inserts side-eye emoji.) So you see, on one hand, I was fighting to get into medical school to make my father proud, but on the other hand I was also trying to figure out what my true passions were.

Ultimately, I never got into medical school. I was hanging by a thread to fit into that world and neglecting my strengths: my creativity, leadership skills, and 'goofy' nature. While I will always love the study of the body and the information that helps us take care of it, I never really wanted to spend my life being a doctor. Now, I don't seek my parent's will or anyone else's. I only want what's in God's will for my life.

Free from other people's expectations of me, I started to do what I really enjoyed.

During the summer of 2014, I hosted the red carpet for the Miss Ghana USA Pageant in New York. It was my first time hosting an official red carpet. I had a blast and my loved ones said I was a natural. My father told me he was happy I was doing what I really wanted to do and actually admitted verbatim that he was "glad I didn't go to medical school". If you know my father, a rigid African man, you would know that's a very big deal!

I encourage you to decide what life you want to live and make it happen. That was an example of a hard decision I had to make in my life. You might have something totally different going on—something that might seem 10x harder to quit than it would be to hold on. It might be a long-term relationship that you know deep down you shouldn't be in. It might be a job to which you've dedicated a great deal of time. Whatever the case may be, your situation always seems harder when you are in it.

Even though it may not seem like it, there's always a way out. The Bible has a lot of lessons and promises that you can use for advice and motivation. Mark 11:24 says, "Therefore I tell you whatever you ask for in prayer believe that you have received it and it will be yours." 1 Corinthians 13:4-8 reads, "Love is patient, love is kind. It does not envy. It does not boast. It does not dishonor others. It is not self-seeking or easily angered. It keeps no record of wrongs. Love does not delight in evil but rejoices with the truth. It always protects, trusts, hopes, perseveres. Love never fails."

Use your network to hold you accountable. Your local pastor or youth minister is waiting to help you. He or she doesn't even have to know you. Go to someone who will give you sound advice and hold you accountable—not your girlfriend who's always encouraging you to make bad decisions. Find the person who motivates and inspires you to better yourself. The person who pisses you off most of the time because you know they are probably right and you just don't want to do what they are advising you to do. If you don't have anyone to turn to, find a local pastor (you don't even have to be a member of the church). Just find someone who has a heart for Jesus and has your best interest in mind. Ask them for advice on reaching your goals and let them hold you accountable.

Weed out the bad in your life, whether food, people, activities, or anything else. Once we get ourselves out of the situations that are keeping us from living the lives we want to live, we have more freedom to create those lives for ourselves. Being a member of a church definitely makes it easier to be held accountable for your actions. You can find comfort and confidence in knowing that your church family members will give you sound advice. And you can volunteer with your church body and attend different events that will leave you feeling fulfilled while you are separating yourself from bad habits that you want to get rid of.

Before we move on, let's recap. Figure out what you want. Write down your goals. Make changes to achieve them. Use your network to hold you accountable.

Scriptures referenced:

1 Corinthians 6:18-20 - Flee immorality. Every other sin that a man commits is outside the body, but the immoral man sins against his own body. Or do you not know that your body is a temple of the Holy Spirit who is in you, whom you have from God, and that you are not your own? For you have been bought with a price: therefore glorify God in your body. NASB)

Mark 11:24 - "Therefore I tell you whatever you ask for in prayer believe that you have received it and it will be yours." (NIV)

1st Corinthians 13:4-8 - "Love is patient, love is kind. It does not envy. It does not boast. It does not dishonor others. It is not self-seeking or easily angered. It keeps no record of wrongs. Love does not delight in evil but rejoices with the truth. It always protects, trusts, hopes, perseveres. Love never fails." (NIV)

CHAPTER 4

PEACE BE WITH YOU

Some people are best loved from afar.

There was this guy (let's call him Kweku) who I thought would become my "perfect little African prince". But we just weren't compatible. Even after we stopped prolonging our 'flirtationship' and went months without talking, I would still check on Kweku via social media and pray for him whenever he would come to mind. We didn't hate each other. We just didn't want to waste each other's time. You see, it wasn't a you're-my-ex-boy-friend-i'm-going-to-stalk-your-life-and-pray-God-brings-you-to-your-right-mind-while-I-pretend-I-don't-care deal. It was more like a you're-still-a-good-guy-and-i'm-going-to-keep-in-touch-but-not-get-too-close-cause-i'm-guarding-both-of-our-hearts-cause-you're-not-my-MOG deal. MOG, meaning man of God.

See, Kweku was my ride or die. You know, one of those guys who it didn't necessarily work out with but you all are on okay terms so you will always show love. I have a few of those guys whom I love like family, but that doesn't mean they will always understand that. They might be wrong for you but are still 'supa fine'. When that supa fine man is in your face all the time, the 'wrong for you' part might get a little fuzzy. So instead of trying to be in their face and risking your own vulnerability, just love them from afar. Keep it healthy. Make decisions with Jesus and yourself in mind. There are some people you have to love from afar-far. Stop. Block. Pop, lock, and drop them out of your life until you are strong enough to resist temptation.

If you know that he isn't for you, let him go. God has someone better for you and someone better for him. Have faith and don't block your blessings. We are all trying to see what the "exceedingly and abundantly all that we can imagine or hope for" looks like. Love yourself enough to make wise decisions boldly. If that means you have to go to a few amazing church services by yourself because your friends won't go, then go! You can't wish for people what they don't wish for themselves, but you can pray for them and lead by example. Don't ditch your old ones but find new ones who share your interests.

Love yourself enough to make wise decisions boldly.

Be careful of the people that you allow in your life. "God is not the author of confusion, but of peace—as in all the congregations of the Lord's people." (1 Corinthians 14:33) If you are not sure if someone belongs in your life, then get on your knees and seek God. If you are on the fence about something, guard your heart. Love yourself and the people around you enough to be strong in your decision-making! Don't be so timid that you miss your blessings. Remember there are many instances where the Bible says to be bold. God will put signs and people in your life to help you make confident decisions. In 1 John 5:14 it says, "This is the confidence we have in approaching God: that if we ask anything according to His will, He hears us". How excellent is that? You know what you deserve. You know how you should be treated. You are worth the Wahala. So don't settle. Love yourself!

According to the friendship average method, you are the average of the five people you spend the most time with. If you have four awesome friends who motivate you to stay on the right track and encourage you to be productive with your time, you are blessed. Bae will come along to complete the puzzle!

With each space in your top five, you have an opportunity to bring someone into your circle of friends who will make your average go up or bring it down. So be careful when deciding who to add to your top five. Yes, I said be careful with your decision, because it's a choice, your choice. Do you want bae to bring down your average or bring up your average? What does your boyfriend or the guy you're talking to now do in his spare time? What characteristics will he offer to your top five? **Will he bring your average up, not change it, or take it down?**

If your boo is always in the club, never reads his Bible, and barely goes to his church on his own, then he will pull your average down from where you want it to be. No matter how hard you try to come up with excuses for your man, think of the tendencies he had before you were in the picture.

Was he making money in a legal or illegal way?

Did he have a steady job and keep his house clean?

Don't forget about his spending habits.

Does he possess qualities that you actually want to rub off onto you?

If he is lower than your average, do not let him drag your top five down. You have to take an unbiased look at him as a person and think about what type of person you want to be and the qualities you want to embody. The 'deadbeat credit card scamming VIP-junkie' that goes to church but never obeys anything that the Bible says is not going to do anything except bring that score down. We don't want that Felecia!

Then there's the guy who won't bring your average up or down—it just stays the same. I don't think this type of person comes by too often because people are generally passionate about their lifestyles. Simply put, this guy will keep you going on the same track. He will be better than the guy who drags you down, but he won't necessarily bring your average up.

How many of us remember having assignments in school where the teacher gave us the option to earn extra credit? I sure do. I used to take every opportunity to get extra credit. Guess why. I wanted my average in the class to go up! The boo you add to your group who keeps the average the same isn't going to get you the extra points you want and guess what? You deserve those points!

When I say you deserve to add someone to your top five who will bring your average person up, I don't mean you need to become friends with Michelle Obama, Paul Washer, Beyonce, Chimamanda Ngozi Adichie, and my dad. I'm saying that you need to add people who have great character traits that you admire and would want to embody.

My fab five are amazing.

I probably speak to my little sister more often than anyone else in the world. She's girly, wise, smart, and stylish. I spend hours in stores sending her pictures of every single item that I consider purchasing every time I go shopping. But I don't mind because her stylishness rubs off on me.

I've known my childhood best friend since 8th grade and she's like the most radical Christian I know. She can be a little weird and over the top at times, but I'm so proud of her for being so passionate for Christ. She inspires me to not be lukewarm but to instead be a light and an oddball to society. She encourages me to reject society's definition of cool, and instead say to myself, "they don't have to think I'm cool. It's God who will decide if I go to heaven, not man." She also worked at a vitamin shop for 4 years so she shares healthy tips and recipes with me too! She sends me sermons, scripture, and inspirational Instagram posts every day. Even though I don't watch every sermon, try every recipe, or take all of her advice, she still rubs off on me and is an important part of my average.

My bestie from college is more of a wild child who motivates me to live life to the fullest. She's a model who loves working out, so I call her if I want to have a good time or need some workout advice. She is an amazing businesswoman with strong project execution skills. She encourages me to get things done in my business and entrepreneurial endeavors.

My friend from young adult's ministry and I met right after we graduated college. She is another great Christian. She inspires me to be non-judgmental, full of love, and totally committed and faithful to Christ. She's in medical school so she makes me smarter too. We used to study together both in college as well as during 'the MCAT grind' after graduating.

Side note: I scored one point higher than her on the MCAT when we took it for the first time and since she got in medical school…technically, I got in too! Right? Y'all, I don't care if you try to hate on me and say that doesn't count! One of my happiest moments in life was finding out that I made that one point higher than her on the MCAT. Just let me have my moment. Anyways, this friend adds to my intellect and faith.

I also spend a lot of time with my roommate so she is also part of my top five. Despite being four years younger than me, she's super hardworking, keeps the house clean, and acts like a granny (just like me). If I lived with someone who turned up all the time, hosted pre-games every weekend, and had different guys over every night, eventually I would come down and have a drink. She would influence me. Because my roommate is super clean, I learn new cleaning techniques from her. And because I'm always cooking, she also cooks a lot more now and tries my unique and healthy recipes. We influence each other in the home.

If I lived with my parents, my top five might be different. I might make more smoothies because my parents make smoothies every morning. I'd probably be like 15 pounds heavier because my parents also eat out all the time and don't work out. (Those things have happened to me by the way!) The people you surround yourself with influence you.

I've talked about my little sister, my childhood bestie, my college bestie, my after-college best friend, and my roommate. While I love my roommate, she's not a solid part of top 5 because her influence may end when she or I moves. Let's say we move apart and I have one open spot to fill in my top five. What if I allow some guy into my top five who curses all the time, is always depressed or angry, and doesn't obey the Word of God? What if I allow him to enter my heart?

If I began to spend more time with him, I'd start compromising with him, because relationships are all about compromise. I'd let him listen to his hip-hop radio station while we are in the car, even though I only listen to Christian radio when I'm by myself. Eventually I'd start changing the dial to the radio stations that I wasn't listening to before. I'd let him curse and, even though I would try not to, I'd start cursing. I'd start getting depressed and hot tempered because I would pick up these tendencies from him. I'd get pulled down and my average would fall below what I truly want for my life.

Righteousness is what we should long for. It is what we need and it's what God wants for us. It's only right. Think about it. That's the root word of righteousness—'right'.

What does someone who will increase our average look like?

He is dedicated to his relationship with Christ, perhaps is even a leader in his church. If he works out and eats healthy that would also increase my average. However, I think that the most important increase to my average would be someone who respects my life in Christ and recognizes my worth. I think that type of man would make my own journey easier because he would realize that his future wife is worth the wait. The man who would increase my average must be someone who wants holiness for me. He must be someone who not only wants me to go to heaven but actually helps me in the journey to get there by motivating me to be strong and not give up.

When I think of someone who will bring my average up, I think of running a marathon. After the 25th mile, you're going to be a little tired. (As a matter of fact after the 25th foot, I'm gon' be a little tired!) After that 25th mile when you have just one more mile to go, you look ahead and see a genuine face smiling and telling you to keep pushing, to go just a little further. He tells you that you can do it. He's done it, so he knows. You finish the race faster than you would have on your own because your partner knew what he was doing and was one step ahead telling you that the way was safe. He gave you that little boost of momentum you might not have had if you had gone it alone.

I want my man to tell me that the way I'm going is safe and right with the Lord. I want him to encourage me. Now imagine you are trying to drag him through the marathon. Your raggedy man is behind you in the race and you had to fight tooth and nail just to get him to support this good cause. He's running the race and keeps asking you to quit and stop at every fast food restaurants he sees.

Wahala. And not the good kind.

Not only does he look a hot mess running a marathon in baggy jeans, but for the millionth time you are yelling at him: "NO, you are not going to quit the race to stop at Checkers!" He is so irritating. You are the leader in the situation and this man who you have allowed in your top five is making your journey harder. Now I don't know which image you all like better—having an encourager or a deadweight—but the fact that I saw a Boris Kodjoe look alike as my man in my first illustration isn't the only reason I chose daydream number 1 as my top five add-on.

You want a partner who will lead you toward your goals not away from them. So make a good choice. Surround yourself with people who bring your average up. Loving yourself and knowing your worth means that you have to make loving decisions for yourself. Sometimes we have to put aside temporary benefits for long-lasting happiness.

If you don't get anything out of this chapter, remember: "Do not be deceived. Evil companions corrupt good morals." (1 Corinthians 15:33)

Scriptures referenced:

1 Corinthians 14:33 - "God is not the author of confusion, but of peace—as in all the congregations of the Lord's people." (NIV)

1 John 5:14 - "This is the confidence we have in approaching God: that if we ask anything according to His will, He hears us". (NIV)

1 Corinthians 15:33 - "Do not be deceived. Evil companions corrupt good morals." (ESV)

CHAPTER 5

SHE USES HER POWER FOR GOOD

So now that we know we possess a wealth of value - what are we going to do with it? How are we going to use this information? We know we are children of God. We know we are worth the Wahala. We know our purpose is to do good deeds. We have identified and come up with plans to get what we want out of life. We are working to better ourselves while letting go of negative influences that are bringing us down. So now what?

You know those sappy social media birthday posts we send to our beloved girlfriends every year? I remember getting one from a very special sorority sister. She said a lot of nice things but one part of her post really resonated with me: "No other person I know can entertain a room full of hundreds of people just by being herself, and she uses her powers for good lol!"

How amazing is it to have someone recognize your gifts and then note the fact that you are using them for good?! We all want to be applauded for our actions, but when someone applauds what you have done and adds that you did it for the good of others without cue, that is a great feeling. All I have ever done was try to live a life that was pleasing to God. The positivity that I share with others is from God. The confidence I have when walking into a room comes from God. I know that I'm in the house to do my Father's work no matter what the event has been planned to promote and regardless of what my role or job description may say.

During a tour I organized showing young adults from America my sweet country of Ghana, I spoke at a local school where I encouraged over 200 Ghanaian students to know their worth and make good investments in themselves. Afterwards, a member of the tour group said that he was happy that I was spreading a good message because the talk was so captivating he would have done just about anything I encouraged him to do. I remember thinking to myself, "Wow, I'm powerful." I understand why my sorority sister made a point to say that I use my "powers" or influence for good.

Once you know your worth, you need to identify your gifts then use them for good. My power happens to be entertaining and encouraging others. Now maybe you can't entertain people because you haven't perfected the craft of being a complete goof, but that's probably a good thing. However, you do have gifts, (everyone does) which you can choose to use for good, for bad, or not at all.

J. Moss has an amazing song "We Must Praise" that says:

If I were a drummer, I would use my cymbal

If I were a writer, I would use a pencil

I would use my voice, if I were a singer

No matter who or what we are, we must praise

If you are unsure of your powers, ask your close friends or family what skills or positive traits you have. Sometimes our loved ones notice things about us that we don't notice about ourselves. Your power may be listening, artwork, or writing. I want you to use your powers for good. I want people to applaud you for doing good deeds with the gifts that God has given you. However, it is important to be content regardless of whether people recognize you or not. It may be a long time before you get the recognition you deserve, but doing good is self-fulfilling and God will reward you. Let's say you're doing great things, but your close network isn't there to support you. They might not even show up until much later when you no longer need their help. Manage your expectations of people. Just because you give 100% to someone doesn't mean that they will give 100% to you. Do not let that change how you value yourself.

Keep moving forward. When it's done, the right people will be beside you. One of my sisters once shared a quote with me that I have come to love: "Passionately pursue what you know to be right. Don't bow down to your circumstances." I would also add 'use your powers for good' along with that passionate pursuit. This is one of my all-time favorite quotes and I constantly replay it again and again in my mind.

Let's be real. It's much easier to use your powers to please society and get instant gratification. Sometimes we are quick to become enamored by what we think is good and beautiful, when it really might not be what's best for our personal journey. Consequently, it's important that we, personally, use our powers for good and guard our hearts from being easily influenced. It's easy to see something on TV and envy it. It's easy to listen to a song and feel pressured to sin. You might have an amazing figure and want to show it off to the world, because we all know Instagram loves a big booty. Guess what? Instagram likes won't get you into heaven, chale!

In Ghana, women wear beautiful beads around the waist. You can find these waist beads on all women from toddlers to the elderly. The beads symbolize beauty, but they must be kept private. Even my 93-year-old grandmother wears waist beads and I've only ever seen them once in my entire life. If a man comes to my husband and says he has had an affair with me, my husband will only believe the man if he knows what color waist beads I wear. Our bodies are beautiful and they are filled with treasures. We live in a society where seeing is believing, but waist beads are an example of beauty that exists that doesn't need to be showcased to the world. We don't have to prove to the world that we have beautiful bodies, we can keep them covered and sacred for who they are intended for! This does not just apply to your body. If the bank teller doesn't know that you have a college degree, does that mean that you don't have one? If the person sitting next to you at the nail salon does not know you are a successful business owner, does that mean that you are not one? We do not have to prove ourselves to anyone. In America especially, we always feel the need to prove ourselves to others. Continue to work hard, but remember you do not have to prove yourself. The only person we should live for is Christ. In Galations 1:10 it says, "For am I now seeking the approval of man, or of God? Or am I trying to please man? If I were still trying to please man, I would not be a servant of Christ." Remember we can't earn what God has in store for us. We inherit it. Why? Because we are children of God. What he has in store for us is already for us. Continue to work tirelessly for what you believe in and remember you don't have to prove yourself to man. You are working for a higher power! I challenge you to wear your invisible crowns and hide your waist beads. Your body is a powerful tool, use it for good.

You have gifts that influence people around you to do things that are either good or bad for them. Do you recommend food that you know you and your friends shouldn't be eating? Do you scream, "TURN UP" every Saturday night and encourage your friends to drink until they drop? Do you laugh and motivate your girlfriend to have carefree flings with guys who are 'only good for the sex?' Think about how amazing it would be if you said, "Hey guys let's chill tonight at my house. I want to go over some scripture with you all tonight!" What about if you stopped having sex before marriage and encouraged your friends to stop with you and become your accountability partners?

What are you producing from the seeds that you sow into your friends and community? Keep working on what you know is good and do so tirelessly. Don't say, "how come I don't have a man, or can't afford all these designer things like those girls?" Your reward is coming, and that's all you need to be worried about. God, who created the sun and the moon and your beautiful, intricately made self, has amazing things in store for you.

You can't look at someone's face or clothing and see their past. You can't even see their present. You can't read into their lives. A news report surfaced about two sisters who were living lavishly from money received after having relations with and then blackmailing married men. It's so easy for us to roll up on someone's page and envy what he or she has based on what we see on the surface. Comparison is the thief of joy. Comparing yourself to other people can easily send you down a depressing path.

Passionately pursue what you know to be right.

When we look at a girl who knows how to perfectly contour her face, we see beauty and someone who seems to have the keys to success in life. Why is showing off the body praised when we know we ain't got no business doing that? When we do what we aren't supposed to you might end up with a top-selling record or enough money to finance your designer shoe fetish, but none of that changes the fact that we aren't supposed to be doing it! God sees the beauty that we can't see. He sees the beautiful, shy girl who doesn't get much attention but has an amazing hidden gift. He sees you. Use your gifts for good. It doesn't matter if you do a good deed and no one sees, or if you have a million people watching you, stop living for the world and do good.

Comparison is the thief of joy.

What if we all used the powers that we have, in the little ways we can, for good? We can all influence people in some sort of way. If you know your friends aren't as healthy as you, encourage them to eat right. Don't just watch them feed themselves junk. Invite them to workout. Invite them to church.

If I have a shopping problem, but don't unsubscribe from the mailing lists of my favorite stores, I will have daily reminders and updates about all the shoes I want, but don't need. Unsubscribe from the temptations, even if they aren't evident at first. Do you see how easy it is to follow someone whose background information you don't know? We look at something for an instant, decide whether it's good or bad, then go on to like it, screenshot it or keep scrolling. We have to be careful about what we take in as much as we are about what we put out.

What you allow in your body and atmosphere control your sense of peace. So eat real food, read the Bible, and listen to e-books that are empowering. As much as I love Waatse, Red Red, okro soup, kenkey, fish and shito, or my friend's Nigerian Egusi soup, I have to have control over how much food I put in my body. Listen to classical music or make other small changes to your daily activities to control your space and peace. The decisions you make whether good or bad will have an effect on your sense of peace. I don't follow anyone on social media that I feel will affect my morals negatively. I don't watch ratchet videos or read vulgar posts because those influences would affect me down the line. I even have to be careful about what music I listen to because too much rap music starts to weigh on my soul. Too much R&B makes me want to sin.

When we are healthy and clear-headed, we can spend the energy (that would have been wasted on that boy 'doing good in the hood') effectively to pursue our goals. President Obama only wears gray or blue suits to pare down decisions so his energy is focused on making clear and decisive plans for the country. He said in an interview with Vanity Fair: "I don't want to make decisions about what I'm eating or wearing. Because I have too many other decisions to make." Similarly in *The Life-Changing Magic of Tidying Up*, Marie Kondo shares that many of her clients became more productive, more organized, wealthier, and some even lost weight by simply getting rid of unnecessary clutter in their homes and offices. I definitely recommend the book. Love yourself enough to de-clutter your brain, your home, and your relationships.

In the Parable of the Pharisee and the Tax Collector (starting at Luke 18:9), Jesus asks us to remain humble as we try to live pleasing lives for Him. Think of the tax collector as the famous Instagram girl I mentioned earlier, and the Pharisee as me. If I'm boastful and proud, I will not be exalted. We should always remember that we are Christ's heirs but never forget that God wants each of us to have a heart of a servant. 1 Peter 5:5 says, "Likewise, you who are younger, be subject to the elders. Clothe yourselves, all of you, with humility toward one another, for God opposes the proud but gives grace to the humble."

Psalm 37:4 says "Delight yourself in the LORD; And He will give you the desires of your heart. Commit your way to the LORD, Trust also in Him, and He will do it."

You have amazing gifts to give to the world. Use those powers for good.

Scriptures referenced:

Galations 1: 10 "For am I now seeking the approval of man, or of God? Or am I trying to please man? If I were still trying to please man, I would not be a servant of Christ." (ESV)

Luke 18:9-13: "To some who were confident of their own righteousness and looked down on everyone else, Jesus told this parable: "Two men went up to the temple to pray, one a Pharisee and the other a tax collector. The Pharisee stood by himself and prayed: 'God, I thank you that I am not like other people—robbers, evildoers, adulterers—or even like this tax collector. I fast twice a week and give a tenth of all I get.' But the tax collector stood at a distance. He would not even look up to heaven, but beat his breast and said, 'God, have mercy on me, a sinner." (NIV)

1 Peter 5:5 - "Likewise, you who are younger, be subject to the elders. Clothe yourselves, all of you, with humility toward one another, for God opposes the proud but gives grace to the humble." (ESV)

Psalm 37:4 - "Delight yourself in the LORD; And He will give you the desires of your heart. Commit your way to the LORD, Trust also in Him, and He will do it." (ESV)

CHAPTER 6

DON'T BELIEVE THE LIES

Now you've got a new mindset, strengthened your confidence, and highlighted positive influences in your life. Everything is great. Right?

Wrong. Is it ever that easy?

Your ex-boo, who just doesn't get it, is going to keep calling you. Your friends still want you to stunt, ball out, and party hard like there's no tomorrow. Sadly, trying to please society doesn't fit well into the life you need to live. It's going to be hard and people may have a funny way of expressing their feelings towards change.

That guy in the store is still going to try to holla' at you. He doesn't know that you are trying to better yourself and strengthen your relationship with God. He simply sees a girl who just dissed him. He thought that the greeting, "Hey, sexy" was endearing. As a matter of fact, learning how to deal with men can be a factor that can make this transition very difficult.

Some men will say any and everything to make you think that what you got ain't worth gold. Lies Felecia! They are so hurt after you dis them that they'll try to make you feel lame or whatever else to transfer their negative emotions onto you. But you aren't even trying to hurt anyone's feelings! You are actually doing them a favor but their immaturity won't let them appreciate it. I've had guys tell me that I'm "regular" and "nothing special". While it would be great if they actually felt that way (because maybe then they would leave me alone!), they're usually just having a hissy fit because I said I wasn't interested.

Some guys will either hype you or hurt you based on whether they think they'll get an ego boost out of it. My close guy friend, who went from promiscuous frat boy to amazing brother and promoter of the King, told me the most interesting thing about guys. Apparently, guys are just as shocked as girls are when they realize that they don't like a girl anymore after they've had sex. The male population can't determine whether they are "in like" or "in lust" until their lust is no longer an issue.

I've had so many guys claim to like me who suddenly stop pursuing me once they found out that they weren't getting 'the goods'. Looking back on those relationships, all I can do is thank God that He didn't allow me to give in to temptation. However, many of us have not been as fortunate to see a man through before giving him the goods, have suffered heartbreak (or worse), and on top of that, now have to deal with a lifelong yearning for sexual pleasure. As a virgin (bomb dropped), how can I explain exactly how non-virgins should deal with those urges while trying to abstain from sex until marriage?

This is my answer: I won't.

I left this difficult task up to my very best friend, Mish. My best friend who had two kids and then became celibate, I might add. Yep, that's right, the girl who is responsible for teaching me how to "twerk" back in middle school—before we even called it "twerking"—is going to set you up for success.

Mish (short for Michel'le) grew up in Hartsville, a small town in the middle of South Carolina. Pretty much, if you don't leave town after high school, you will have a baby. There's just not much to do other than to be in a relationship, get into small-town drama, and go to high school sports games.

In high school, she was a popular honors student who was a co-editor of the school newspaper and involved in student government. We graduated; everything was great, and then bam! Sometime between graduation parties and walking across the stage, she got pregnant. We were all shocked. She gave birth to my goddaughter (her baby shower was fab—I planned it) and two years later, bam! We get word of another one. This girl done got pregnant again. After doing things her way for a little while, she got saved, moved back in with her mom, and hasn't let any more men in her bed. And plans to keep it up until marriage.

She is a real life inspiration. She meditates on God daily. Her love for Him is the most beautiful thing I've ever seen. She is like no other Christian I've ever met and I learn from her every single day (whether I want to or not). So I asked Mish, what advice can she give to people who want to abstain from sex until marriage. She said:

First, hide the Word in your heart so that the supernatural power of God can help you resist.

Secondly, don't put yourself in compromising situations. Sometimes books and movies that talk about sex put you in compromising moods. There's no 21-day fix. It's by His Grace.

And the last piece of advice, you have to FIGHT LIKE HELL.

I agree with Mish—avoiding compromising situations is key. Certain friends might be included as some of those "compromising situations". When you surround yourself with others who are truly about that life, you will work as a team together to reach your goals.

When I asked Mish for tips to help us say no to the day-to-day temptations we face, she was steadfast on encouraging us to store the Word of the Lord (ie. The Bible) in our hearts. I had already written her life story, hyped her up and was expecting her to just come with a bomb list of all the things she does to be an amazing Christian. But to my disdain, Mish kept saying: keep the Word of the Lord stored in your heart.

I wanted and needed more. Many of us are looking for something to help us through the real struggles that we face. Many of my friends come to me for advice on how to actually live the life God wants them to live. When it's 2 AM and you're feeling that 'after dark temptation', you aren't going to want to pull out your Bible.

In fact, you might actually pull out your Bible and still sin right after. One time, I yelled scripture at my friend as she left our slumber party to go visit her ex. She still went. I prayed for her after she left my house. That didn't change the fact that I didn't see her until the next afternoon. It's hard and I don't have the magic potion. I assumed Mish did. But in actuality, we can't do anything without God.

I was reminded of this through a close friend who was going through a difficult breakup. She had no interest in her daily activities as she was overcome with sadness and fatigue. But, her minister gave her some amazing advice: listen to the audio Bible during workouts, cleaning around the house, and driving. She told me that within a week she felt herself getting back to normal.

It can be hard to move on when you love someone's potential and are comforted by the memories of good times you shared. Rest assured. God is a gracious God. If He tells you to let it go, there is a reason. Trust Him. Just like Mish and my friend going through the breakup, no matter how strong you can be, we all have weak moments and we can find strength is in the Lord!

How about we all wait until marriage to give up the goods? Let's do it! If a man is willing to stick with you and sacrifice for you until your wedding day, you know that your relationship is built on more than lust. Many of my friends tell me that they could never wait to have sex until marriage because they want someone to enjoy their body, they want to enjoy sex, or they want to preview what they are agreeing to spend the rest of their lives with. But how many of us have heard stories of people staying in relationships just for the convenient sex? Ladies, isn't it so sad that we might be missing out on our own God-given Boris Kodjoe because we are dealing with our freshman boo from college?

Stay focused on your goals and not on the lies of the world by investing in yourself. An investment is defined as the action or process of investing money for profit or material result. There are several ways you can invest in yourself. One way is by reading a good book. Books are filled with knowledge that is either so interesting or so important that someone spent nights on end crafting their project so it would one day become a small object designed for your reading pleasure. People don't write books because they woke up one day and wanted to work hard. They write books because they think they have great ideas and feel compelled to share.

I am writing this book because I find myself saying things over and over again that I want to share with a great number of people. I want women to be confident and to know their worth. I'm just an amateur trying to get a message across. Think about how amazing the Bible is. Think about how awesome history books are, economic empowerment books, and every other book that might strike your fancy.

Speaking of economic empowerment, invest in yourself by becoming financially literate. There are lots of great books and programs that will teach you about the game of money and how to manage your finances. (I recommend David Ramsey's Financial Peace.) Strengthen your budgeting skills. Learn how to invest in stocks and mutual funds.

Go to the gym. Learn how to sing. Take up an adult dance class and learn how to salsa. Obsess over the Food Network and take a cooking class. Go to an art gallery. Find an amazing piece of art. Take a painting class and make a signature piece for your dining room. Figure out how to do your hair (especially if your friends keep telling you to do something with it). Find your favorite bra types. Make yourself a fantasy wardrobe and start saving up to bring it to life. Learn how to play an instrument. Teach yourself how to knit. Start your own business. Learn a new language. Stretch in the morning before you start your day. Get your best friend to teach you how to make her famous whole lemon-butter chicken. Volunteer at a local outreach program.

If you are hiking, meditating, and eating amazingly healthy homemade foods then you are giving yourself the best of what God wants for you. If you don't have a job to pay for any of those things, there's always YouTube. Teach yourself. Also, invest in a resume, and go get yourself a better job!

Live Life! Live it. Make yourself better and invest in yourself. We waste so much time talking on the phone to people who are no good. We waste so much money trying to be cute in the club for no-good players who still live with their mothers. We waste way too much emotion on great people, who just aren't great for us. It's time that you start valuing your time and spend it on someone who deserves it without a doubt: you!

While it may seem easier said than done, there are a lot of ways that you can keep yourself encouraged while you stay away from evil. Creating a personal encouragement statement has motivated me. What is your personal encouragement statement? There's a young Jamaican trainer on Instagram who uses the phrase, "Strength! No weakness... mi nuh do weakness!" I've used it during workouts and it works! He says it all the time and, while it's entertaining, it actually works. Next time you're in the gym and you don't want to finish your set, just tell yourself, "Strength! No weakness!"

We waste way too much emotion on great people, who just aren't great for us.

One night several years back, I came home from a party where I had been drinking and acting out of character. I got home, looked in the mirror, and asked myself, "Who am I"? Who was the girl in the mirror? Who was she trying to be? I stripped down to just my skin. I wanted to get rid of the 'world' that was on me. I wanted to beat the lies that told me this—the partying, drinking, and acting wild—was what my life was about. The world wanted me live a life of partying and party girl façades, but that wasn't what Jesus wanted for me.

I took off all the jewelry that I could in my drunken state. (My ring and earrings were a little too hard to take off with my acrylic nails so I had to settle with what I could, but you get the point). I wiped off my makeup and washed my face. I looked in the mirror at the real Borley. No makeup. Nothing extra. I asked myself what I wanted. I wanted to focus.

I got my red lipstick and wrote in big letters on my mirror:

"THE DEVIL IS A LIAR! YOUR LIFE IN CHRIST IS ONE FILLED WITH PURPOSE, DETERMINATION, RESILIENCE AND PERSISTENCE. YOU ARE WORTH THE WAHALA."

That was my personal encouragement statement -just like that in red, bold, passionate print. Those are things that I have to remind myself of every day. Whenever I don't want to do work, I replay that statement in my head. Whenever I'm having trouble figuring out whether a guy is for me or not, I think of the statement.

I said that the devil was a liar because he is. He will try to make you think that life is fine and dandy while you're just going through the motions and not living out God's purpose. But we will end up in hell this way.

The Bible says do not be lukewarm (Revelations 3:15-16).

Jesus wants us to be passionate about what we stand for. Remember that in Chapter 2 we said our purpose on earth is to do good deeds. While the world might not end if we do not carry out our purposes, we will surely suffer serious consequences for failing to follow God's Will. Remember, you have a purpose. You are created with unique talents that the world is waiting for you to use.

I have to remind myself that my life is filled with purpose. I am a sister, a daughter, a co-worker, a friend, a mentor, an entrepreneur, a writer, and so much more. I'm a singer and a dancer too (just not outside of the confines of my home). I'm whatever I want to be and my life has purpose. The Bible tells me that I'm a co-laborer with Christ (1 Corinthians 3:9). So I have work to do. We all do. From working at a drive-thru window or on the executive board of a huge consulting firm, we can all use our earthly jobs to bring glory to the Kingdom. What is your purpose? Remind yourself and work to fulfill it. Remember your purpose.

I have to remind myself to be determined. I have to be determined to work on my projects every day, even if just a little bit at a time. If I want to learn a new language, I have to be determined to work on it even when I'm tired and don't have the energy. I have to be determined to stay away from exes who don't have my best interest at heart even when I feel lonely and want companionship. I have to be determined to

Remember your purpose.

eat right and workout regularly because I know that my body is a temple and I'm worth the hard work. I have to remind myself to be determined and that my life in Christ is filled with determination so that I won't sit at home on the couch doing what's easy: scrolling through Instagram. **Be determined.**

I have to remind myself to be resilient. The enemy will come at you like a flood (Isaiah 59:19). Guys will try to bring you down. Customers, bosses, and co-workers will try to bring you down. Even, the guy on the street who is asking for money will try to bring you down if you catch him on the wrong day. It is HARD to live a life in Christ. If it were easy, everyone would be doing it. We are humans. We make mistakes. We have to thank God for grace, but work hard to obey His Word. You have to be resilient to fight through the hard times.

My trainer always says that your gains are made at the end of the workout. On the last set, when you are worn out and ready to slap someone or give up, you have to push through. In the beginning, it's easy to have great form. It's easy to make a Snapchat video of you working out on the first set. You have your matching neon purple athletic gear. You haven't dripped a drop of sweat yet, your edges are still on fleek, and you are ready to show your snap followers that you are at the gym. By the end of the workout, you don't even know what the word "form" is. You are just happy to be standing upright. Your hair is a hot mess and the only thing you are concerned with is leaving the gym ASAP.

However, you can't leave. That's when the change happens. You have to be resilient. You have to push through. Breathe. Focus on your form. That's when the change happens. When you are tired and ready for bed but you stay up an extra thirty minutes to study for next week's test, that's when the change happens. When you really want a deep-dish pizza from Lou Malnati's in Chicago but you decide to eat your bag lunch, that's when the change happens. When you are sad because you want companionship but you don't give in to your ex, that's when the change happens. When money is tight but you don't break any laws or compromise your morals to make ends meet, that's when amazing change happens. **Be resilient.**

I have to remind myself to be persistent. After motivating yourself to be purposeful and determined while fighting through hardships as the resilient star that you are, you have to keep going. You have to be persistent. You might fail a few times along the way, but you have to keep going. You have to keep working towards your goal. **Be persistent.**

I remind myself of all these things because I am worth the Wahala. I'm a child of God. My name is special in my Father's eyes. Someone loves me and He loves you too. He thinks you're amazing and He created you to be worth the Wahala. You are so worth it!

Think of a mantra and write it down. Say it to yourself as often as you can. Your personal encouragement statement may change every few years or months. At one point, I was suffering with feelings of insecurity in busy, public places so I reminded myself that, "I'm a happy, loving, and confident bombshell". I proclaimed dominance in areas of my life where I needed to reassure myself. That way, when the world tried to tell me who I was, I already knew the truth. This isn't narcissism; it's reverse psychology.

I find that when you take the time to think about what kind of encouragement you truly want, you can make a personal encouragement phrase that will benefit you in the best way possible. Nobody knows you like you, so take the time to create a statement of encouragement for yourself. Remember, your personal encouragement statement may change after you've convinced yourself of it. Also, remember that you should keep some statements to yourself. I would never post online that I am a "confident bombshell". This is just something I do to encourage myself. Always stay confident, but remain humble. Humility is a beautiful gift.

I also pray. *The Prayer of Jabez by Bruce Wilkinson* changed my life. It was one of the books my mother would buy me and my siblings for Christmas that we would kick off to the side. (Side note: Another one of those books that I absolutely loved was *The Purpose Driven Life by Rick Warren*.) Anyways, when I got a little more mature, I would find these random books, read them, and love them. I thank God for my mother and for her heart. It's unfortunate that I didn't appreciate her sooner, but sometimes God's plans for us are slow coming.

I say the prayer from *The Prayer of Jabez* multiple times a day—maybe ten times minimum. Often times, I'll find myself singing it in a song when I'm off in la la land. Whenever I need God to change my heart or to give me strength, I pray this prayer. It has really and truly changed my life. You have to read the book. (It's all of like 50 pages long so go read.) I've even tried to figure out how the prayer is so bomb by deciphering it and creating new prayers with its same components. The prayer goes like this:

"And Jabez called on the God of Israel saying, 'Oh, that You would bless me indeed, and enlarge my territory, that Your hand would be with me, and that You would keep me from evil, that I may not cause pain.' So God granted him what he requested."

This exact prayer came from Jabez in the Bible, who God thought was the "most honorable" (1 Chronicles 4:9-10). You have to read the book to get a breakdown of how saying this prayer will really change your life. Just like some people say the same prayer every time they have a meal, you can have a strength prayer like this to use when times get rough. You can also make one up yourself, like you did with your encouragement phrase.

Keeping ammunition (or ammo) on you will keep you strong when society tries to tear you down. That's right, it's about to get real. We are at war. The Bible says in Ephesians 6:11-13 to "put on the full armor of God, so that you can make your stand against the devil's schemes. For our struggle is not against flesh and blood, but against the rulers, against the authorities, against the powers of this world's darkness, and against the spiritual forces of evil in the heavenly realms. Therefore take up the full armor of God, so that when the day of evil comes, you will be able to stand your ground".

The devil is going to try to mess with our spirit. He's going to try to make you overthink things, be anxious, feel lonely, and have bad days. He may not necessarily send someone to shoot you, but he will find a way to bring down your spirit. His actual aim is to disrupt our relationship with God. That's why it's important to stand firm in the Word. When you have the Word of God in your pocket, you have Jesus Christ with you at all times. He is the Word (John 1:1). This is why it's important to memorize scripture. Scripture comes in handy in the most inexplicable ways.

I hope that you've been writing down all the scriptures thus far that have really encouraged you in the notes section in the back of this book. When you have a list of Bible verses and spiritual ammo, you have God fighting with you. The Bible is filled with encouraging promises that God wants us to remember.

I have used the following three scriptures to fight all my battles.

God is a God that will not lie. Numbers 23:19 says, "God is not human, that he should lie, not a human being, that he should change his mind. Does he speak and then not act? Does he promise and not fulfill?"

What we decide on will be done. Job 22:28 says, "What you decide on will be done, and light will shine on your ways."

He knows His plans for us. Jeremiah 29:11 says, "For I know the plans I have for you," declares the LORD, "plans to prosper you and not to harm you, plans to give you hope and a future."

God is good and He has proven His love and graciousness to His people throughout the Bible and, as the great Tye Tribbett says, "If He did it before He can do it again."

We are at war but we are well equipped. We have the armor of God. Ephesians 6:16-18 reads: "In addition to all this, take up the shield of faith, with which you can extinguish all the flaming arrows of the evil one. And take the helmet of salvation and the sword of the Spirit, which is the word of God. Pray in the Spirit at all times, with every kind of prayer and petition. To this end, stay alert with all perseverance in your prayers." Make sure you break down your war gear and equip yourself with all the tools that you will need to fight off the enemy.

When we have ammo, we can get through adversity.

When I pray for my friends, I'm not praying that they won't go through any adversity. I pray that they will be at peace during the hard times and come out on the other side as a champion. What doesn't kill you makes you stronger. If we never went through any hard times, we would be spoiled and useless. Sometimes a little wear and tear equips us with the tools we need to be even better than we were before.

Several months after buying my house, my realtor came over to see how I had turned this once empty potential home into my now most cherished personal investment! I showed him an entryway console I bought from Goodwill that I was trying to transform (I had fallen in love with DIY projects!). While the console was absolutely beautiful, with a lovely finish, I needed to paint it to make it match the color scheme of the rest of my house. My realtor told me that I needed to sand down its exterior to make sure paint would stick. He let me know that if I tried to paint over the console as it was, the project would fail.

Sometimes we need some 'sanding down' in order to come out better than we were before. Sometimes when we feel a little resistance, we are able to turn that pain into something beautiful. In life, you can count on going through some sort of trial or tribulation. Knowing this, I want all of my friends and family to face adversity head on so that they can celebrate the stronger people that they will become when their problems pass.

Repeating scripture to yourself is a great way to stay calm while being 'sanded down' by situations in life.

God is not the author of confusion. (1st Corinthians 14:33)

He won't put more on you than you can bear. (1st Corinthians 10:13)

Ask God for wisdom to help you conquer your situation. He'll give it. (James 1:5)

They are powerful tools to use in sticky situations. Use scripture in your life like you use food. You will feed the Holy Spirit living inside of you, you will see amazing changes in your actions, and blessings will come your way. If you have questions about your gut feelings (the Holy Spirit which lives inside of you), ask your local pastor. Keep the Living Word active inside of you! Scripture, scripture, scripture!

As you walk in your calling, don't believe the lies that this world has waiting for you. Remember, you are royalty. You are always wearing an invisible crown. You have mantras, prayers, and ammunition locked and loaded ready to fight off any negativity trying to steal your joy.

DJ Khalid was right.

They don't want you to be great. But *they* gone' learn today!

Scriptures referenced:

Revelation 3:15-16–"I know your deeds, that you are neither cold nor hot. I wish you were either one or the other! So, because you are lukewarm–neither hot nor cold–I am about to spit you out of my mouth." (NIV)

1 Corinthians 3:9–"For we are co-workers in God's service; you are God's field, God's building." (NIV)

Isaiah 59:19–"So shall they fear the name of the Lord from the west, and his glory from the rising of the sun. When the enemy shall come in like a flood, the Spirit of the Lord shall lift up a standard against him." (ESV)

1 Chronicles 4:9-10 - "Jabez was more honorable than his brothers. His mother had named him Jabez, saying, "I gave birth to him in pain." Jabez cried out to the God of Israel, "Oh that you would bless me and enlarge my territory! Let your hand be with me, and keep me from harm so that I will be free from pain." And God granted his request." (NIV)

Ephesians 6:11-13 - "Put on the full armor of God, so that you can make your stand against the devil's schemes. For our struggle is not against flesh and blood, but against the rulers, against the authorities, against the powers of this world's darkness, and against the spiritual forces of evil in the heavenly realms. Therefore take up the full armor of God, so that when the day of evil comes, you will be able to stand your ground". (NIV)

Numbers 23:19 - "God is not human, that he should lie, not a human being, that he should change his mind. Does he speak and then not act? Does he promise and not fulfill?" (NIV)

Job 22:28 - "What you decide on will be done, and light will shine on your ways." Jeremiah 29:11 - "For I know the plans I have for you," declares the LORD, "plans to prosper you and not to harm you, plans to give you hope and a future." (NIV)

Galatians 6: - *Entire chapter*

Ephesians 6:16-18 - "In addition to all this, take up the shield of faith, with which you can extinguish all the flaming arrows of the evil one. And take the helmet of salvation and the sword of the Spirit, which is the word of God. Pray in the Spirit at all times, with every kind of prayer and petition. To this end, stay alert with all perseverance in your prayers." (ESV)

John 1:1 - "In the beginning was the Word, and the Word was with God, and the Word was God." (NIV)

1 Corinthians 14:33 - "For God is not a God of disorder but of peace—as in all the congregations of the Lord's people." (NIV)

1 Corinthians 10:13 - "No temptation has overtaken you except what is common to mankind. And God is faithful; he will not let you be tempted beyond what you can bear. But when you are tempted, he will also provide a way out so that you can endure it." (NIV)

James 1:5 - "If any of you lacks wisdom, you should ask God, who gives generously to all without finding fault, and it will be given to you." (NIV)

CHAPTER 7

WHAT OTHER PEOPLE THINK OF YOU IS NONE OF YOUR BUSINESS

Contrary to popular belief, what society thinks of us does not matter.

However, certain people have been placed in our lives for specific reasons, like your church pastor or a friend who has become your accountability partner. So, if your college roommate wants you to try drugs and thinks you're a punk for saying no, that doesn't matter. But on the other hand, if your prayer group thinks that you are spending too much time with your boyfriend to the point that you are slacking on your commitments to God, that should matter to you.

We place people in our lives for different reasons. Some friends can be the angels on your shoulder; other friends might be the devils. That's why it is important to choose the people whom you spend the majority of your time with very wisely. Sometimes you think someone will be a good fit for you but later find out that they are not. The hard part is making sure you separate yourself from these ties before they influence you in the wrong way.

We should always be focused on the end goal, as it is the only thing that really matters. And that end goal is Heaven (to kick it with Jesus). As Christians, I believe, and the Bible says, that we should strive to live Christ-like lives and to always glorify His Name with our actions. When our times on earth end, we want to be welcomed into Heaven! That means we need to make disciplined decisions now. So when we find ourselves in situations that seem out of our control, we need to press forward and remember that the end goal is the ONLY thing that matters.

You don't have to be cool in the eyes of society to be happy with life. In my opinion, it's actually more stressful to try to keep up with the Jones'. Stay clear-headed and worry about the things that matter, such as showing love and bringing people closer to God. My grandmother once told me "loving someone is wanting the best for them and if you want the best for someone, you want them to go to heaven." Love others how you would want to be loved. Empathize with and love on other people as you would want someone to do for you if you were in their shoes. Love your brothers and sisters of this world. Love them and share the gospel of Jesus Christ with them.

Be strong in the face of pressures from this world. Make wise decisions and always do what's right and good. Most importantly, always remember the end goal.

You are an heir of the Kingdom. You deserve the best.

But what is 'the best'?

In this day and age, it's easy to confuse what looks best and what makes you feel best with what is best. If you can't tell by now, this book seeks to break down the lies of popular culture and reveal truths.

When I say I want the best, people often ask me, "So, what kind of guy is your type?" Usually followed by something like: "I mean, would you date someone who works on cars?" My answer—YES! Of course I would date a guy who works on cars. Do you know how to fix cars? I don't. It would be amazing to have a man that can fix your car instead of having to go to mechanics and worry that you might get bamboozled! Besides, I would love to watch a man fix my car in the heat of the summer as I sit under a tree and sip lemonade. Maybe it's a South Carolina thing. Nevertheless, a little part of me thinks that people want me to say "No, I would never date a car mechanic". Yet, I have no qualms with the idea.

There are lots of things that I would love for my significant other to be able to do. For instance, I don't like using remotes, setting up technology, or installing hardware in my house. A handy-man bae would be a great companion in my life because he would complement skills that I lack. A lot of people automatically assume that a potential boo is only 'next level' if they work in corporate America. However, that couldn't be further from the truth.

See, there are lazy drunkards, abusers, and cheaters in suits and in corner offices all around the world. There are car mechanics who spend sleepless nights working tirelessly on business plans with dreams of opening up their own shops. There are also magnificently smart corporate men working hard, living faithfully, and investing valuable time in their families. And at the same time, there are 'aspiring musicians' who are really just aspiring to stay at their mom's houses and play video games. I say all this to say that it's not about what you do, it's how you do it.

The type of man I want is faithful to God and his loved ones. He is confident, ambitious, a leader in his family and community, charming, and loving. If he has his character traits downpat, he can easily work as a cashier in a cafeteria. Why? Because, if he is ambitious he isn't going to be lethargic. Each of his moves is calculated—even if one of the moves is in a cafeteria—and that is what should matter to you.

Society says that if a guy has money and a good job, he's the one. No. Throw that way of thinking out of the window. Does he bear good fruit? Does he invest in you? Does he make you feel secure? These are the determining factors. These are the kind of questions that you should be asking yourself. At the end of the day, you are going to be the one who endures the emotional consequences of being with this person who will directly impact you every single day. **Choose wisely.**

If you got into a relationship for the wrong reasons, reevaluate the reality of the situation. Pray about getting to know the real character traits of that person. See if the relationship is in God's will for your life. You deserve the best, not some guy playing shakara with your heart because you think he has a nice car.

You deserve someone who is as loving as you are. You deserve someone who puts in as much energy and time as you do. This is what I mean when I say you deserve the best. The best does not have to equal seven figures—that's just icing on the cake.

Think about why you are doing what you are doing right now. Are you in a master's program in order to become more qualified for your dream job? Are you taking an audio language course so that you can connect with more people in the world? Are you working at a daycare in hopes of one day opening your own or to dedicate time so that you can secure the manager spot? That same ambitious guy who works at the cafeteria cash register could be the future owner. He could be training in each position to make sure he is aware of all of his future employees' tasks.

So what kind of guy is my type? Trust me, there's a long list I created during my year of reflection and purposeful singleness. Some things are absolutely necessary like being a Christian who will lead me. Others are less significant (but I had to put them in the air) like having muscles. God says that He will give you exceedingly and abundantly all that you can ask or imagine (Ephesians 3:20). Write down what you want out of your significant other and pray over it. Make sure you are not being shallow in what you are asking God for, but don't sell yourself short either.

Make your list 3D. Did you write down that you want a man who is caring? What does it look like to have a man who is caring? Maybe it's someone who asks how I am doing or helps me pursue my dreams. Write those things down as well. I tell people all the time, I will be single until I am 81 years of age before I settle. If you know me, you know I mean it. You should be happily single and waiting until God blesses you with your MOG (man of God)!

Scripture referenced:

Ephesians 3:20 - "Now to him who is able to do immeasurably more than all we ask or imagine, according to his power that is at work within us." (NIV)

CHAPTER 8

SEX IS FOR MARRIAGE

I know I've already lost some of you just from the title of this chapter, but I want you to really embrace what will be discussed in the coming pages. Please don't skip past this chapter, it's very important.

In modern society, sex is everywhere. It's on our televisions, in our movie theaters, on our radio stations—and in our relationships.

It's also in our Bibles! The Bible tells us that sex is for marriage. Consider 1 Corinthians 6:18-20, which says, "flee from sexual immorality." Some of us think that waiting until marriage to have sex is just an antiquated law in the Bible that doesn't apply to modern society, but guess what...it does.

Sex is not for your boyfriend of seven long years. It's not for your 'dream guy' who you are 'pretty confident' you will marry. Neither is it for your fiancé or God forbid your casual here-and-there hook ups. Sex is for marriage. Sex is for after you tie the knot. Sex is for after you have officially married someone, and not a moment sooner.

Many people ask me, "What if I wait until I get married and the sex is whack?" My response to that is: do you think that if you waited to be joined together with the person whom GOD wanted you to be with—someone who turns you on mentally and physically and who just clicks with EVERY aspect of your being—you would be let down in the intimacy arena... by God? The Bible tells us that God will give us exceedingly and abundantly more than we can ask or even imagine (Ephesians 3:20).

If you ask for and imagine your husband to be wonderful in every way, do you believe God will give you something less than your wish? I had this same conversation with one of my girlfriends and she kind of brushed it off. However, almost a year later, while on a tour of Ghana with Afoko Adventures, several of the tour participants got prayed for, including my friend. She bashfully told the group after the event that her leg had never shaken the way it did while in the assembly hall after being prayed for. She was comparing being filled with the Holy Spirit to sex. God wins every time!

God gave us sex because He wants us to do it. However, He wants us to do it right. Sex is a form of honoring God. When I'm married, I plan on honoring God as often as humanly possible. Chale, we gon' honor God from sunrise to sundown! In fact, I know of a church in North Carolina that gives newlyweds stripper poles as wedding gifts. Now, some people don't like the idea of getting a stripper pole from your pastors but chale, I'll gladly accept mine!

Regarding every nook and cranny of life, we are called to put our trust in God. The Bible promises that we do not have to worry about what tomorrow will bring because tomorrow has enough worries of its own. The Father who created the lilies in the valley, will He not clothe you who He made in His image?" (Matthew 6:34). Don't worry about the future. Worry about making sure that your life is in alignment with God's Word. Find a spouse who wants the best for you—heaven. Be a potential spouse who wants the best for your lover—heaven. By doing these things, you will both motivate each other to remain abstinent until marriage.

Today, many think that we are to be abstinent for marriage. Instead, we should realize that we are abstinent until we are married. We are abstinent for God. If you find the man you're going to marry and say, "Ok we'll be married so we can have sex", that's the wrong mentality. You can only (and I mean only) have sex AFTER you have been married.

If you know you are going to marry someone, go get married. What's stopping you? Is it the wedding planning, finances, or guest list? None of those are good excuses. Go get married in a court if you must, but keep it under wraps until the big day. But until you are married, you aren't supposed to be getting boogie, in any way!

According to the Centers for Disease Control & Prevention, half of all marriages end in divorce. That's five of your friends if ten of you lined up together! However, think about how that rate would decrease if couples decided to commit to each other before the marriage. And if they tested each other's true love and commitment to God. Wouldn't each person have a better idea of the man or woman of God that they plan to marry? They would surely weed out some bad eggs, and that's not in vain.

We might not understand it, but there is a reason why Jesus calls us to remain abstinent before marriage. It is something we are supposed to do as Christians. So why is it that it is so common for believers to ignore this rule?

It is a sin. And sinning can be tempting. Just like eating an extra bite of food when you know that you're full. That's a sin too, right? Gluttony. While tempting, there is no good reason why someone should talk you out of abiding God's law. There is no amount of good behavior your lover can show that is worth disobeying God. He got you flowers, so what? You deserve to be treated like the daughter of the Most High King. THE MOST HIGH KING! That's your father, and guess what? You are worth the wait.

I can't say this enough: you are worth everything. You are allowed to abstain from sex and leave your lover if they get mad about it. Remember, a man is supposed to love his wife as Christ loves the church. That means he should love you passionately. He should love you so much that he would take the initiative to save you–to lead you to heaven. He needs to help you, not hinder you, in your journey.

Reflect on your relationships–past or present. If you told your man, "Babe, I want to live a life that's pleasing to God, and want to know how you would feel about abstaining from sex until marriage." What would he say? If you're currently in a relationship, ask to find out. If you explain the root of decision and how important it is to you, he should agree to abstain.

He should try to keep you strong (and vice versa). That doesn't mean to reward him with sex for agreeing. Just like you are not abstinent for him, he's also not abstinent for you. You are both abstinent for God. So don't stay over too late. Don't hang out alone for too long. Proverbs 28:26 says, "Those who trust in themselves are fools, but those who walk in wisdom are kept safe." Set yourself up for success, by planning ahead and not putting yourself in compromising situations. If either of you start to feel desires, you both need to run far away! It's going to be hard, but God won't put anything on you that you can't bear (1st Corinthians 10:13).

And chale a beg, I never said abstaining would be easy for anyone, especially the people who have already experienced sex. The light at the end of the tunnel is that suffering for God is a good thing. For instance, Psalm 15:4 says God honors those who keep their word even when it hurts! In James 4:7-8 it says, "Submit yourselves, then, to God. Resist the devil, and he will flee from you. Come near to God and he will come near to you. Wash your hands, you sinners, and purify your hearts…" And that's where most of us stop reading, but lets keep reading. Verse 9 and 10 says, "**Grieve, mourn and wail. Change your laughter to mourning and your joy to gloom**. Humble yourselves before the Lord, and he will lift you up!" Chale! It's right there, plain as day. It's going to hurt.

It's going to hurt.

I remember a time I was talking to someone I had no business talking to. Every chance I would get, I would go and see him. I remember asking God to just tie me up and stop me from going to see this guy. If I had the option, I was going. I knew it wasn't right but I just didn't feel strong enough to resist. That's when a friend brought up the two scriptures I mentioned above and reminded me about Adam, Eve, and the forbidden fruit. This was practically the first story in the Bible and God told Adam and Eve not to eat fruit from one tree in the garden. Life was easy for Adam and Eve in the garden.

Everything else other than the forbidden fruit was fair game. And what did they do? They ate the fruit. A serpent in the Garden tempted them. Now if it were me, I would have said "Lord if you don't want me to eat the fruit from that tree, can you just remove it?" But that's not how it works. There's a reason why this was one of the first lessons in the Bible. It illustrated that God will provide us everything we need to succeed, but when He says not to do something, we shouldn't do it. The temptations might be right in front of us, but that's inexcusable. You have to find a way to be strong through the grieving, mourning, and wailing that comes along with doing what's right. Now, if that 'aint Wahala I don't know what is, but you are worth it!

We are supposed to enjoy sex—but only in the confines of marriage. So go out there and let your MOG (man of God) find you! Make sure God gives you the OK, and then get married. Then, have all the you-know-what you want! Let's say it one more time for good measure – Sex is for marriage!

Scriptures referenced:

1 Corinthians 7:2 - "But since sexual immorality is occurring, each man should have sexual relations with his own wife, and each woman with her own husband."(NIV)

Ephesians 3:20 - "Now to Him who is able to do immeasurably more than all we ask or imagine, according to His power that is at work within us" (NIV)

Matthew 6:34 - "Therefore do not worry about tomorrow, for tomorrow will worry about itself. Each day has enough trouble of its own." (NIV)

Proverbs 28:26 - "Those who trust in themselves are fools, but those who walk in wisdom are kept safe." (NIV)

1 Corinthians 10:13 - "No temptation has overtaken you except what is common to mankind. And God is faithful; He will not let you be tempted beyond what you can bear. But when you are tempted, He will also provide a way out so that you can endure it." (NIV)

Psalm 15:4b "...who despises a vile person but honors those who fear the Lord; who keeps an oath even when it hurts, and does not change their mind;" (NIV)

James 4:7-10 7 Submit yourselves, then, to God. Resist the devil, and he will flee from you. 8 Come near to God and he will come near to you. Wash your hands, you sinners, and purify your hearts, you double-minded. 9 Grieve, mourn and wail. Change your laughter to mourning and your joy to gloom. 10 Humble yourselves before the Lord, and he will lift you up. (NIV)

CHAPTER 9

LET THEM GET THE TICKET

When I was a kid, I would ride in the car with my mom and cars would always speed passed us on the highway. I would get so annoyed. Sitting shotgun on these extended rides, I would look at the passing cars, the speed limit signs, and then my mom's odometer. "Really mom," I would say, "All the other cars are passing us." Her response was always, "Let them get the ticket."

Inadvertently, my mother was teaching me not to change my actions simply because of other people, but instead to stay focused on what was best for me. The same idea can be found in the commonly used phrase, "Stay in your lane".

Now, let's delve into how staying in our own lane can help us. How many times have you seen someone coming up fast from your rearview mirror and all of a sudden you press on the gas a little? You say to yourself: "They aren't about to pass me." No one wants to be the slowest person on the road. We don't want to get left behind. And so, without knowing it, we let the cars in other lanes influence our own journey.

You should know the difference between positive and negative influences in your life. When she was travelling too low under the speed limit, my mom would sometimes need a little reminder to get her to pick up the pace. I think this is positive influence. Your positive influences help you to effect change. They bear good fruit in your life. On the other hand, let's say that you are going the speed limit and cars pass you by, so you speed up to well over the speed limit. These cars are now influencing you to break the law. These are bad influences. Focus on eliminating the negative influences in your life and stay in your straight and narrow lane.

I remember stepping out to an alumni party and running into a peer who found out that I would be traveling a lot for my new job. He told me to go out and 'sow my royal oats'. Interestingly, out of all the things he could have told me, that was his great advice to make the most of my new career. I tried to think of a socially acceptable way of playing it off as I didn't agree with anything he said—at all, in any way—but, I didn't want to start a long drawn-out conversation in a loud crowded bar, so I left it alone. Looking back I probably should have used that opportunity to let him know that I'm not that kind of girl and nobody else should be either. (There are definitely fun ways to say things like this without sounding like a buzzkill.)

Like that random person and his unsolicited advice, there is always the chance that someone might say something which can cause you to look into someone else's lane. For example, you are caught eyeing the chocolate display by a grocery store cashier who laughs and says, "YOLO". But you know you shouldn't have one because you are on a diet. Personally, it's not out of my character to be like *shrug*, "ok," and grab it (especially if it's buy one get one free!). I'm weak and I struggle with staying in my own lane. People, whether close family, friends, or even random strangers, can always influence me.

I've learned that life is harder when we surround ourselves with people who we love, but don't necessarily agree with. However, just because they believe something doesn't mean we have to believe it too. And just because they want to do something doesn't mean we have to do it too. This is where 'staying in your own lane' starts. God doesn't want us to be totally free from everyone in the world. We couldn't, even if we wanted to (1 Corinthians 5:9-11). But He does want us to stay faithful to him and true to our beliefs. When your best friend wants to have sex before marriage and encourages you to feel free to do the same, stay in your own lane.

I bought my first house in a quiet, up and coming area of Atlanta when I was 25 years old. I love my city and when I meet people from around the world, the one thing they know about Atlanta is Buckhead. In New York City, it's Manhattan. In Accra, it's East Legon. In London, it's Kensington. In Atlanta, Buckhead is known for it's high end shopping and fine dining. First, people ask me where I live, and then they ask me where it is in relation to Buckhead. I've even had coworkers give me concerned looks when I tell them that I live twenty minutes south. There's nothing wrong with my quiet community, but as a young professional, I rarely find my counterparts choosing to live in my hood. Why? Because they all want to live in Buckhead! And I don't blame them. Buckhead is nice, posh, and convenient. You, living in Buckhead is like people looking over in your 'lane' to see you driving a Mercedes G550! Imagine the smiles and affirmations I would get from co-workers, friends and people I meet around the world if I could say I lived in Buckhead too. No Wahala. I could have gone the Buckhead route, but I didn't. Instead, I decided to buy a house on the edge of the city and live with a roommate. It wasn't the cool thing to do nor the most socially acceptable for someone my age. I have to drive twenty minutes to be a part of the action. I have to schedule my own gutter cleaning appointments and hire my own handyman. But I didn't want to put thousands of dollars in the hands of an apartment owner that I would never meet when that money could be going into my bank account. I decided buying a house and living away from the city (in one of the only houses I could afford) was worth the Wahala. I decided to build equity, invest in myself, continue my journey to being debt free and put in the work. My father once told me that you should work hard in your youth so that you can enjoy the fruits of your labor in your mature years. A lot of us never learned that concept. We feel entitled to live a luxury life after doing little to no work, simply because we can. As much as I would have loved to live in Buckhead, I knew that wasn't what was best for me at this time. For those that have already reached that level, more power to them! Their path might be different than mine, however, it doesn't mean that we can't get to the same destination. I know that one-day, I will have the Benz, the Buckhead condo and more. I just have to work hard and stay in my lane. It's worth the Wahala!

Re-evaluate your current path. What is the Buckhead in your life? Are you making the best decisions for yourself or are you living to look good for others. In today's world, we want to enjoy the moment, and we rarely consider the future. Don't risk a better future for the present flex.

Comparing yourself to others influences you. It makes you behave like you are driving on Ghana highways (nobody stays in their own lane). Sometimes when we aren't focused on our own blessings, we get caught up admiring everyone else's. But we don't know what that person had to go through to get to the blessing that we are envying. We don't know God's intentions for giving certain blessings to that person and not to us. This can apply to material things, relationships, family members, talents, promotions, and more.

Once you define your lane, stay in it. Throughout this book, we have discussed the importance of knowing what you want, and not settling for anything less. We must pray to have the strength to stay in the Bible, in prayer, and committed to our goals. People around you might seem like they are speeding past you and not working as hard, but stay focused. If you are driving down the road and going the speed limit, you are on track. While someone may speed past you now, you might pass them a mile down the road as they receive a ticket from the cops.

When I see humble, hardworking, and honest men, I see men with characteristics I would want in a future husband and father to my children. However, we have been trained to look for nice cars and athletic builds instead. For the longest time I wondered how the clubbers-without-jobs pulled off the VIP sections and bottles every weekend. Then I found out that many of those "flexers" were credit card scammers. It was very naïve of my young, innocent mind to think they were making legitimate money. So why do we want to entertain men who could end up being our pen pal in prison?

Jesus was so humble. Why do we have to go for the loudest, flashiest guys in the room? When we know we are in the right lane and that the right people are also in that lane with us, we don't feel like we need to change our actions. We won't feel bad when we don't speed up because everyone else is passing us. You don't have to go 25mph (please don't be that guy) nor 65 mph in a 45mph zone.

The fact of the matter is that a lot of people allow themselves to be negatively influenced. Shoot, you might be allowing it. You deserve better. You actually deserve better than what you think you deserve in even your most perfect dream of a love story. You deserve to be your strongest, most stable, and most loving self. You deserve a relationship with a man who is all of that and a bag of chips (if a relationship is what you desire).

For every person you sleep with, you are adding a soul tie that you may or may not know right away affects you. Why can't we take pride in enjoying our bodies and saving them for our future husbands, who will enjoy the fact that it's all for him?

The only thing that has come from sexual relationships in my lifetime has been hurt. One girlfriend of mine recently allowed her ex back in her life after a year of not seeing or thinking of him. The moment he left after their "reunion" she felt a deep wave of depression overcome her. We have become programmed to think that sex and intimate relationships are necessary because everyone else is doing it. We have slowly forgotten how to rely on ourselves for love. We have forgotten how to count on God when we are lonely. We have forgotten how to make lasting friendships with both men and women.

So how can we stay in our own lanes in a world where everyone around us is saying, "jump in mine", "swerve into his", and "matter of fact, lets all share a lane for the night"? The Bible even says stay in your lane—just in different words. Deuteronomy 28: 13-14 says, "The Lord will make you the head, not the tail. If you pay attention to the commands of the Lord your God that I give you this day and carefully follow them, you will always be at the top, never at the bottom. Do not turn aside from any of the commands I give you today, to the right or to the left, following other gods and serving them." If focusing on what's going on in your life is not enough to help you from falling under the pressures of society, just keep reading through to Deuteronomy 28:15 when the Bible expounds on what happens to you when you don't obey the word.

You need to focus, and trust me, chale, it will be hard.

Scriptures referenced:

1 Corinthians 5:9-11 - "I wrote to you in my letter not to associate with sexually immoral people– not at all meaning the people of this world who are immoral, or the greedy and swindlers, or idolaters. In that case you would have to leave this world. But now I am writing to you that you must not associate with anyone who claims to be a brother or sister but is sexually immoral or greedy, an idolater or slanderer, a drunkard or swindler. Do not even eat with such people." (NIV)

Deuteronomy 28:13-15- "The Lord will make you the head, not the tail. If you pay attention to the com-

mands of the Lord your God that I give you this day and carefully follow them, you will always be at the top, never at the bottom. Do not turn aside from any of the commands I give you today, to the right or to the left, following other gods and serving them. However, if you do not obey the Lord your God and do not carefully follow all His commands and decrees I am giving you today, all these curses will come on you and overtake you." (NIV)

CHAPTER 10

LOVE VS. LUST

I know a lot of people say that 'love is pain' as if heartbrokenness is a normal part of love and intimate relationships. Even my own sister has unconsciously said that love was pain while speaking to me, I immediately thought to myself: "no it's not!"

The Bible says that "Love is patient, love is kind. It does not envy, it does not boast, it is not proud. It does not dishonor others, it is not self-seeking, it is not easily angered, it keeps no record of wrongs. Love does not delight in evil but rejoices with the truth. It always protects, always trusts, always hopes, always perseveres" (1 Corinthians 13: 4-7). So why is it that whenever I reflect on my past relationships, I feel hurt and heartache? It turns out that I didn't really love those guys like I thought I did.

See, lust is the doozey. Lust is what we don't want. Lust feels like an addiction. It's the feeling that you get from your 'loved' one where they cause you pain but you still want to go back to them so they can make it feel better. Why would you go back to the same person who hurt you, to make you feel better? Because we love them and lust for them.

I love Sam Smith's song "Stay with Me" because it illustrates these emotions perfectly:
"Oh, won't you stay with me?
'Cause you're all I need
This ain't love, it's clear to see
But darling, stay with me

Why am I so emotional?
No, it's not a good look, gain some self-control
And deep down I know this never works
But you can lay with me so it doesn't hurt."

Why do we stick with certain relationships when we know deep down that they won't work? Lust will give us a pained feeling even when the person we are lusting after isn't for us.

God hates lust. One of my pastors once told me that you can't go north and south at the same time. We love what God hates. He hates sin. But we sin to make ourselves feel better when we are hurting. "Stay with me!" "Lay with me!" We beg our partners when we should be begging God to stay with us and to lay with us so we don't hurt. He will take away the pain. Pain, people. Love is pain when it's done the wrong way. I don't know of anyone who can say they haven't experienced pain from the idea of love, rejection from love, or longing for love. It's a powerful emotion.

Imagine what love would feel like with YOUR man? Your MOG who is all yours. He is someone who God has been meticulously planning your past, present, and future to mold you for. Imagine God working hard to put that MOG in situations to cultivate within him leadership skills and a great work ethic so that he is able to provide for your family. Imagine that man loving you, and you loving him, faithfully out of reverence to Jesus Christ. Imagine desiring your husband and being attracted to him. Imagine experiencing great gifts from God in your marriage with your MOG, and only your MOG. Those thoughts don't evoke pain. They evoke bliss, fresh love, and newness.

Even though we write down what we want in a relationship, we still need to be careful when looking for those qualities among the choices of men who are available to us. For example, maybe we want a guy who will buy us shoes. Well, the dope boy around the corner has money so we'll talk to him. This is an example of how, despite our good and careful intentions, we can end up with the wrong guys.

Please don't think the 'dope boy around the corner' is only in the hood. Don't play. Y'all know if your man makes money legitimately, whether he's in a corporate office or in a college classroom. Many of us want to talk to flashy guys who, in turn, want the big booty girls and love strip clubs. Meanwhile, the broke, nice boy in medical school doesn't even get a second thought.

Let's keep our emotions in check. Whom are we lusting after? Whom are we allowing to bring us pain? Whom are we going back and forth to? Whom have we been dealing with month after month (or even year after year)? They want to act right, then they get trifling, then they want to act right again, and then they go right back to being trifling. We know the routine. Yet he's still in your inbox, and you still have feelings for him.

Try to discern the difference between love vs. lust. Be strong when you need to cancel out lust interests in your life. One of my Top Five friends (from Chapter 4) gave me some advice when I was down and out that will always stick with me. I was in the middle of getting over an ex and was considering reaching out to him in a time of weakness. After listening to me go on and on about this guy she finally told me, "Borley, sometimes you just have to be a 'G'." I immediately knew that 'G' stood for gangster. She went on to explain that when getting over someone you know is not for you, you have to get into 'G-mode'. When you start thinking pathetic I-want-him-back thoughts, you have to shake them off and ask yourself what a 'G' would do. 'Gs' don't show weakness. A 'G' won't put herself in a compromising situation. And a 'G' definitely doesn't set herself up for failure by associating herself with someone who is going to set her up. So, when you are thinking about texting him that you want him back, think 'G-mode'.

The Bible also tells us to get in 'G-mode', but with a twist. It's what I like to call 'HG-mode' aka Holy Ghost mode. Ephesians 6 in the Bible says we, "aren't fighting against flesh and blood… but against the spiritual forces of evil." Lust is one of those evils. How else can you have feelings for someone who treats you poorly? The Bible says that we should put on the full armor of Christ including "the sword of the Spirit which is the word of God". Aka, get strapped! Sling that sword of the Lord around like an Asante warrior. You have to take the sword of the Lord and swing that thing around you like crazy. In this new season of your life you're going to be participating in a different kind of slay. You are slaying those lustful, weak thoughts right out of your mind. Get in HG-mode.

Scriptures referenced:

1 Corinthians 13:4-7 – "Love is patient, love is kind. It does not envy, it does not boast, it is not proud. It does not dishonor others, it is not self-seeking, it is not easily angered, it keeps no record of wrongs. Love does not delight in evil but rejoices with the truth. It always protects, always trusts, always hopes, always perseveres." (NIV)

Ephesians 6 *Whole chapter*

CHAPTER 11

SINGLENESS

On one, especially lonely, night during my year of intentional singleness, I wrote in my prayer journal:

"I just want to thank You for singleness. Sometimes when I'm home alone (like right now), I wish I had someone here with me, to encourage me, to joke with me. However, in that same instant, I thank God for singleness. It's a blessing to spend time alone working on projects I am passionate about, eating foods that I love, listening to things that move me, and meditating on the things I love.

I thank You, Lord, for this time to be me, and to be with 'me'. I thank You, Lord for this time to be happy in my aloneness, to motivate myself, to find comfort in You, and to focus on the fact that, even at my loneliest, I'm never truly alone. I'm excited for my future, but I'm also excited about my present. I've never been able to be single like this before. I'm single without any wanting to be in a relationship. (I might have said that before but for the past year I have felt and meant it!) How amazing it is to really be alone and to enjoy my aloneness!

God is good. I'm blessed in this moment.

PS I just made this amazingly strange dinner for one with a pound of brussel sprouts, a fried egg with provolone ('cause I was too lazy to scramble it), and some leftover cauliflower curry. I can just about guess if there was anyone else in my house with me that they wouldn't have been down for the cause—except maybe my future husband."

Singleness is a blessing. What if God's plan for your life meant you needed to be single for the rest of your life? In that situation would your listen to God and remain single? I'd say you should.

On average, we have about 81 years to live on this earth so we have a short amount of time to fulfill God's good and perfect Will of bringing people to Him and spreading the gospel. Whether you are single for a phase or for a lifetime, figure out why God has put you in this blessed position and make the most of it. Use it as a time to grow and rely on God. God is there for us when we feel alone. Just talk to Him and He will help you out.

God made our weaknesses just like He made our strengths. If we were perfect, we would not need Him. The Bible says God's strength is made perfect in our weakness (2 Corinthians 12:9), so we can rely on Him to work on the weak areas that we need to improve. Meanwhile, we can use the strengths God has given us as tools to do work for His Kingdom. This way we need Him and we honor Him at the same time. So when you are finding it hard to stop texting that married man, get close with God. (Yeah, it just got real there).

It's kind of like working out. No one wants to go to the gym (or at least no out-of-shape person). It's much easier to eat a carton of ice cream or some waffle fries than it is to get through those first 20 minutes on the elliptical. But once we spend some alone time with God—with no cheat meals or hookups—you will feel fulfilled, with just you and Him (not by stuffing your face with a doughnut)!

As weird as this might sound, I sleep with God. He holds my hand and sometimes we cuddle. I love Him. He protects me from the monsters under my bed even as a 27 year old. Praise Him! I can count on Him to be there for me instead of any of the boys who would love to take that spot. He won't just tell you what you shouldn't do, He will tell you the right thing to do and walk with you. He might say, "no lusting or sexing before marriage", but He's also going to be there for us when we need Him the most. He won't leave us hanging.

Don't rush into a relationship. Don't always feel you need to get love from guys. Be single. Get that love from God. I'm planning and praying that the next boyfriend I have will be my husband. I know what I want and I can't wait for God to introduce me to my best friend.

I won't waste another minute on a guy who doesn't deserve me. I won't settle for a guy who can't match what I'm bringing to the table or would cause me to compromise my beliefs. He's going to have to be the bomb and expect the bomb out of me. He's worth the trouble and so am I, honey. We are worth the Wahala.

Scripture referenced:

2 Corinthians 12:9 – But he said to me, "My grace is sufficient for you, for my power is made perfect in weakness." Therefore I will boast all the more gladly about my weaknesses, so that Christ's power may rest on me.

Chapter 12

COUNT YOUR BLESSINGS

It can be difficult to appreciate our blessings when faced with the problems of life. However, even in the midst of struggle, it is important to take time to thank God because we have been blessed with so much.

The beauty of life is that God created each of our personal life experiences to be uniquely our own. No one else will have the same life experiences, thoughts, or emotions that I have, because my life is my own. Even my family members, who have been with me from the beginning, each have very different outlooks on life. We invite sadness and stress into our lives when we try to be like others. You end up struggling to get a job that 'looks good' to society rather than venturing out on the road less traveled to start that business which would allow you to follow your true passion. Or maybe you might kick a good guy to the curb because you are waiting for God to 'change' your fine ex-boo—when he's your ex for a reason.

If we fit in, then we will be a part of something and then we'll be happy, right? I remember laughing at jokes that I didn't actually think were funny (nor would I ever make) simply because everyone around me was laughing. I remember being the butt of those jokes and hating it in middle school. Why do I laugh? I've gotten better at not laughing, but every once and a while I still give a fake chuckle here and there at the workplace. I laugh at obscene jokes when the storyteller is staring at me waiting for a response. I'm guilty.

When I was younger, I wanted to fit in with the popular

girls because they wore nice clothes and the guys loved them. However, after hanging out with them, I realized that it was more important to surround yourself with people who you enjoy being around, not just people who seem cool from the outside. So I decided to take the time to appreciate the amazing group of friends God had already put in my life by placing my energy in celebrating my relationships.

Count your blessings and always be positive. Wait for God to work your life out in the way it's supposed to work out. Let's appreciate who and what He puts in our lives. After my year of singleness, I thought I knew everything that I wanted in a man. I wanted a man with great morals, but I had shallow requests that I thought God should reward as well. I started off my new year by dating two great guys. One was a businessman, well-mannered, and super sweet to me. The other was an athlete with a great body and strong relationship with God (from the outside). Although the businessman treated me like a princess, we just didn't click. I put him on the back burner to see how things would go with the athlete. (I did this for shallow reasons.) Let me tell you, it was the worst date of my life and I never spoke to the athlete again. I was more worried about being the perfect-looking couple on the outside that I didn't appreciate the treatment I was receiving from a "grade-A" man who's inside was on point. I shouldn't have kicked a great guy to the curb for a six-pack.

Even problems can be blessings because they create opportunities for God to make His strength and faithfulness known to you. A friend of mine was always complaining that she needed a new car as she had been driving the same one around for years. She was clearly ready for something different. One night she parked her car on the street outside of her house. Guess what happened? Someone ran into the side of her car, then drove off. She had to bring her car to the shop and figure out how to get around without a car. However, she used the opportunity as a learning experience. She said that she should have been grateful for having a car at all instead of always complaining about it. Try to count your blessings before you count your complaints.

Challenge: Close your eyes. Take a deep breath, hold for five seconds, and breathe out slowly. Try to feel all the different parts of the body that are keeping you alive and kicking. While you perform this simple act, thank God for them. You are truly blessed.

Challenge: Set a timer for 30 seconds. Write down as many blessings as you can think of (ex. this book, your favorite foods or pastimes, inspirations).

Chapter 13

WAIT ON GOD

I believe that you should wait for God's instruction before acting. This applies to making decisions ranging from big purchases down to even deciding what you will eat for dinner. When we put God in the equation of your decision-making, we will either know right away when something is right, or we will know with time. Our decision-making could take two seconds, two days, or even two years before it feels right, but God's timing is perfect.

God does not rush. So why would He want to rush you when making decisions? I imagine that God makes decisions in a cool, calm, and collected way. Furthermore, I believe that if someone were to attempt to hurry God by saying, 'Come on God, hurry up. You need to decide what you're going to do now or else?', I envision Him sitting there majestically giving whoever said that an unwavering blank stare.

Similarly, we should make confident decisions for our lives. We should never feel pressured into anything. Humans are worrisome. We rush people for our own agenda or sometimes we rush them because we think we have their best interest in mind. Regardless of the reason, until God gives the go ahead, we should always wait for His counsel.

Now this doesn't mean you should put off important decisions because of fear. Sometimes we let fear overpower us and affect our decision-making. Remember, 2 Timothy 1:7 says "we are not created with a spirit of fear, but with a sound mind." God wants us to be bold and take on the world by storm. He wants us to go after ideas that we believe in. He wants us to jump into the missions and assignments He gives us—but, at the same time, you should never feel pressured into doing something.

Let's put this concept into practice. Imagine that you're buying a car and the car salesman is telling you that he will give you the deal of a lifetime, but only if you buy the car today before you leave the dealership. The interest rate is low. The price is marked down significantly from the sticker price, but it's still a little more than your budget has allowed. Even though you were looking for a Honda and the car he is trying to sell you is a Benz, you start thinking that his deal might be great if you were looking for a luxury car. You didn't get the go ahead from God on this. You feel like you need a little more time to research and talk to friends and family, but the dealership is closing in 15 minutes. What do you do?

Here's another one. God tells you to quit your job, sell your house, and move to Alaska to do missions with Alaskan fisherman today. What do you do?

The difference between these two hypothetical situations is that one is instructed by God and the other is man-made. If you are uncertain about the car, don't buy it—no matter what the dealer tells you. However, if God instructs you to do something, do it. We are human, but we shouldn't feel uncertain about when God gives us instruction because we know that He has our best interest in mind. If you are uncertain about whether that instruction truly comes from God, fast and pray for clarity. Ask people from your church and family to pray for you as well.

Sometimes we hide behind excuses so that we won't have to make important decisions, such as: "I don't know the first thing about selling a home", "doing _____ would be way too complicated", or "I'm unsure of what the outcome will be so I'm just going to do nothing." When God tells us to do something, we need to do it. Sometimes He uses our friends or family members, sometimes He tells us directly, and sometimes He just gives us a gut feeling that even though it won't be easy, it's the right thing to do. When God gives us instructions, we shouldn't delay in our obedience. Sometimes we are tested on our timely response to God's instructions.

When God gives us instruction, He wants us to be bold and make daring decisions. But when it comes to man-made decisions and issues (like the car example above), He doesn't want us to be rushed or be unsure. Take your time with life. Don't feel like you have to rush to take opportunities or enter relationships. The Bible says in Revelation 3:8 that when God opens a door, no man can shut it. So when there is an opportunity in your face and you are unsure of what to do, you need to pray and wait until God gives you instruction.

In the past, men have tried to rush me into relationships and intimacy. But I would take a step back, realize that it wasn't something God wanted me to do, and I wouldn't do it. When a guy seems like a great catch, it can be hard to say no. But trust God. He will not put you in confusing situations without the wisdom to find what is best for you. God is not the author of confusion.

My best friend lived in a very small town in South Carolina for decades before God told her to move. She longed to develop her career and live in a more robust city, but God told her to stay in her small town. So instead of moving without the go ahead from God, she became more engaged with her church, started volunteering, and did what she could to make the most of her time in her small hometown.

In that time, she helped to start a small accountability group with some of her high school friends. She encouraged them to strengthen their relationships with God. She learned new techniques for her job and started turning in innovative proposals to her boss on how to increase business. She made the most of what God gave her and eventually she got the go ahead to move. In her new city, she doubled her income and joined a new church where she felt an overwhelming sense of love and community. For the first time in her life, she was independent and enjoying the journey God was leading her on.

So if you aren't sure what God is telling you about a certain guy or about a big move, what do you do in the meantime? Better yourself by getting right with yourself, your community, and the Lord. We can get right with the Lord by praying, reading the Bible, and fasting.

Bettering yourself. While you are in your waiting season, you can find many ways to better yourself and do well in your community. There are three ways I believe every woman should better themselves while they wait for God's plans to come to fruition in their life: (1) get right with the Lord, (2) get right with your community, and (3) get right with yourself.

Getting right with You. Go better yourself. Make friends. Go to church events. Talk to strangers. Pursue a passion. Overcome a fear. Get a great job. Learn to cook. Learn to speak a new language. Re-organize your house. Go and better yourself! We should always be learning, growing, and taking care of ourselves.

Books are our friends. There is a New York Times Best Sellers list for a reason! A lot of people have to buy, believe in, and recommend a book for it to make that list. I recently got a library membership. I can now borrow e-books and listen to them while I clean my house. This is a budgeting tip I picked up while researching about saving and investing money. However, I still love holding a physical book in my hands so not only does my library card cut costs for me, it also saves time and allows me to access an amazing selection of books.

There's a plethora of information we can find when we search the web. One of my brothers, who is into rock climbing, can find tons of climbing centers in his city. And my other brother, who loves bikes, can find special biking shoes and biker meet ups to compete in local races. My younger sister, who loves beauty and fashion, uses the internet to remain in-the- know about things such as smell goods, home teeth-whiting techniques, and the latest fashion trends.

My older sister, who loves interior design, has introduced me to the world of Pinterest (which is basically the handbook to life after the Holy Bible). I love learning about beauty, fashion, and new ways to clean my house through magazine articles, blogs and YouTube videos. There are endless resources that we can use to help us to become our best selves. Whether it's taking a community course on how to buy a house, or joining a local French club to learn a new language, you should spend free time doing fun activities to better yourself. Make use of the resources that God has given you while you are in your waiting season.

Community. Are you a member of a church? Do you volunteer on a weekly basis? Whatever your reasons for not doing it are, throw them out the door. Go and join a church family and become a member! If you are reading this and you are an active member in your church then encourage a friend to become a member. It's a great feeling when you can fellowship with your church family.

Getting right with the Lord. While you are focusing on strengthening your relationship with God, you will start to hear Him clearer. So when He gives you the go ahead to do something, you will have no doubt that you are receiving instruction from the Big Guy. To get right with the Lord, it is so important that we pray, read the Bible, and fast.

Pray. Prayer changes things! And guess what, I think I have the equation for a great prayer! Prayer is the first step towards getting right with the Lord. I wrote down my two favorite prayers and pulled out the similarities. I then used those elements as a guideline for you to create your own unique prayer to God.

Let's start with the Lord's Prayer (Matthew 6:9-13). This is God's instruction for what your prayers should be like.

"This, then, is how you should pray:
'Our Father in heaven,
hallowed be Your name,
Your kingdom come,
Your will be done,
on earth as it is in heaven.
Give us today our daily bread.
And forgive us our debts,
as we also have forgiven our debtors.
And lead us not into temptation,
but deliver us from the evil one.'"

My other favorite prayer is the prayer of Jabez (1 Chronicles 4:10) which we talked about earlier in Chapter 5.

"Now Jabez called on the God of Israel, saying,
'Oh that You would bless me indeed and enlarge my
border, and that Your hand might be with me,
and that You would keep me from harm that it may not
pain me!' And God granted him what he requested."

You'll notice that both prayers had the following elements:

1. Honoring the Father
2. Request for blessings
3. Live right pledge
4. Request for protection
5. Repentance
6. Requests that His Will be done

Using those elements, I came up with my own prayer. You can too. Here's my version, found in Borleronomy 1:1.

'Lord, You are the bomb.com. You are more than the bomb.

com! I pray that before anything else, Your Will be done. I pray that You'll bless me more than I could ever imagine. I pray that You'll forgive me for my past and future sins. Help me to resist temptation. I want less of me and more of You. Use me as Your vessel. I want to live for You. In Your blessed and Holy Name I pray. Amen.'

Read the Bible. It says that you should wear the belt of truth, breastplate of righteousness, shoes of readiness by the gospel of peace. The only weapon you have is "the sword of the Spirit, which is the word of God, praying at all times" (Ephesians 6:10-20). Remember, His Word is ammunition. We are at war and you need to use what you can to be prepared to stand firm "against the schemes of the evil." The Word is more powerful than you think and even listening to the audio Bible in your car on the way to work, or reciting scripture to yourself throughout the day will help you to hear God when He speaks to you.

Fast. In the treasure that is Matthew 6 we get instructions on how to pray and fast! Go read that right now! In a nutshell, pray, read your Word, and fast! In doing so, you will have the tools to get right with the Lord.

Scriptures referenced:

Matthew 6:9-13 - Pray then like this: 'Our Father in heaven, hallowed be Your name. Your kingdom come, Your will be done, on earth as it is in heaven. Give us this day our daily bread, and forgive us our debts, as we also have forgiven our debtors. And lead us not into temptation, but deliver us from evil." (ESV)

1 Chronicles 4:10 - "Jabez called upon the God of Israel, saying, "Oh that you would bless me and enlarge my border, and that your hand might be with me, and that you would keep me from harm so that it might not bring me pain!" And God granted what he asked." (ESV)

Ephesians 6:10-20 – "Finally, be strong in the Lord and in the strength of his might. Put on the whole armor of God, that you may be able to stand against the schemes of the devil. For we do not wrestle against flesh and blood, but against the rulers, against the authorities, against the cosmic powers over this present darkness, against the spiritual forces of evil in the heavenly places. Therefore take up the whole armor of God, that you may be able to withstand in the evil day, and having done all, to stand firm. Stand therefore, having fastened on the belt of truth, and having put on the breastplate of righteousness, and, as shoes for your feet, having put on the readiness given by the gospel of peace. In all circumstances take up the shield of faith, with which you can extinguish all the flaming darts of the evil one; and take the helmet of salvation, and the sword of the Spirit, which is the word of God, praying at all times in the Spirit, with all prayer and supplication. To that end, keep alert with all perseverance, making supplication for all the saints, and also for me, that words may be given to me in opening my mouth boldly to proclaim the mystery of the gospel, for which I am an ambassador in chains, that I may declare it boldly, as I ought to speak." (ESV)

Matthew 6 - *Whole chapter*

CHAPTER 14

SPREAD LOVE & THE WORD

When you are trying to save the world but nobody wants to be saved, it can feel very frustrating. You are literally trying to save your friends from an eternity in hell, but it seems like they just aren't trying to hear it. When this happens, take a deep breath, count from 1 to 10 backwards, and send your prayers up to God. Then, think about how you also used to act. Think about that one girl in school who used to always invite you to Bible studies and church programs, but you never attended.

Yes, you may have re-prioritized and changed your life around, but your friends might not be there yet. So, do what you have always done—be a good friend. Your friends will learn from watching your moves. They will see you become more clear-headed, confident in your decision-making, and blessed beyond measure. Keep praying for them. God might use you to bring them closer to Him when the time is right.

Until then, however, it can be frustrating. I remember wanting my friends to enjoy going to church for fun. No one likes a boring church service, and I guess those were the types of events they thought I was going to. I love a church where I can be myself, have fun, and fellowship. Those are the type of church services I've enjoyed, invited my friends to, or I would even go to by myself. I would send group texts, individual texts, posts, pictures, tags, and almost went as far as to bribing my friends with a pizza party from the trunk of my car, but rarely did anyone join me. I think my girlfriends were always stuck in the "church is going to be whack and I'm going to have to put up a front" mindset. I felt like I was a high school guidance counselor trying to get unmotivated kids to apply for scholarships. I found myself screaming in my mind, "This can help you!" The thing is, my friends weren't down for the cause and again, this frustrated me.

So what do you do?

You keep doing everything we have talked about in this book. Be the best you can be, but most importantly, show lots of love. Loving is just fun. Love your neighbor, your strange co-workers, your grocery store cashier and (yikes) even your enemies. Not only does showing love put you in a better mood, it's also kind of really important to God (1st Corinthians 13).

God says that it doesn't matter how much faith you have or service you do. If you don't have love, you have nothing. Nothing! He gives us instructions on how to love (1 Corinthians 13:4) and He also says that the greatest of faith, hope and love is, of course, love! I'm sure you've heard this many times before but it's always good to review. The Greek language has several words for our one English word 'love'. *Philia* meaning deep friendship, *lupus* meaning playful love, *agape* meaning love for everyone, *pragma* meaning longstanding love, *philautia* meaning love of self, and *eros* meaning sexual passion.

When I talk about love, I don't mean go out and find someone to *eros* with to fulfill your love requirements, especially if you have taken the route of celibacy. I mean we should go out and give some *agape* love. Go out and give an outpour of gratitude and love to your *pragma* peeps. Let them know you are thankful for your long relationship with them and show them love—for no reason at all. I want you to go out there and *philautia* yourself. Yes, you have my permission to a lifetime of #shamelessselfies. As my sister always says, "#selflove is important".

Let's not catch each other being mean. Don't be a bully. Being petty doesn't fall in the love guidelines. Do good. Let's fill our schedules with loving people who will love us back. Let's love ourselves enough to commit to cutting drama out of our lives. Let's surround ourselves with people around us who respect our decisions. I want you to look at life from a different lens. I want you to have hope in your future and faith in the journey that God is walking you through. I want you to do what is right, never bow down to your circumstances. God is love and you are loved. Go out and be a light. Show people what love looks like. Always remember your crown.

Do you remember the guy from the beginning of the book that asked me, "Why are you causing me so much wahala?" My response, "I'm Worth the Wahala!" was not just to him, but also to the world. You see, I was never "wahala" to begin with. I was only responding to his worldly perception of me. Just because popular cultural has a definition of you, it doesn't mean that its absolute. Sometimes our society thinks that doing the right thing is troublesome or dramatic, but in actuality it's necessary. You are necessary. And while doing the right thing may not be easy, you are worth it! And the peace that comes with doing the right thing is worth it. So as long as *they* continue to think that doing the right thing is wahala, I'm here to say *"wahala dey"* a.k.a this wahala is here to stay!

Scripture referenced:

1 Corinthians 13:4 - "Love is patient and kind; love does not envy or boast; it is not arrogant or rude. It does not insist on its own way; it is not irritable or resentful; it does not rejoice at wrongdoing, but rejoices with the truth. Love bears all things, believes all things, hopes all things, endures all things." (ESV)

ACKNOWLEDGMENTS

This book is for the young girl who feels like she has no one who understands her, loves her, or cares about her. It's for the impressionable girl who is in the middle of a sea of peer pressure. The guys at her school might be the only ones who show her attention. The girls at her school might only accept her if she proves she's crazy enough to do things that they all know they shouldn't be doing. That impressionable girl is one I first met in elementary and middle school. It's a girl who I fought not to be, but at times lost battles to. This book is for that young girl who grew up and who I continuously meet throughout my life: in college, in my corporate job and in my network. Her age has no limits. She is a product of her environment. The purpose of this book is to go into the environment where that girl is and shake it up. The purpose of this book is to remind or introduce her to the idea that she has value. She is worth fighting for.

I want to thank Jesus for putting this passion for that girl on my heart. I just love God. Growing up I never wanted to write a book, but when you live a life for God, you are called to do things you never thought you'd do. I'm thankful for this journey and the relationship that I'm blessed to have with Him.

I thank you for reading this book and for sharing it with 'that girl' in your life. She needs it and is waiting for you to share it with her.

I want to thank all my friends who have been there for me over the years and who have encouraged me when I was that girl. Thank you Amelia, Michel'le, Ket, Kylie, Cynthia, Karra, Aisha, Andre, Peace, Maria, Jada, Afoley, and my brothers. To many more who believed in me and sent me words of encouragement along the way, I appreciate you and you have not gone unnoticed in my heart.

Thank you to my pastors who I have formed close relationships with over the years, who have guided me and encouraged me in Pittsburgh, Hartsville, Accra, and Atlanta!

Thank you to everyone who has an instrumental role in making this project a reality from website and book design, editing and promoting. There are too many people to count, but especially GiGi, Dev, Joy, Micheal, and Maggie. Also Bethany, Derek and Alex, thanks.

To my parents whom I love dearly, I could never repay you (but I will try)!

And again, to my Father and Lord Jesus Christ whom I operate for, I could never have done any of this without Him. I am in a living relationship with Him and He has changed my life. This relationship is available to all and is the one best decision I have ever made in my entire life. It is a gift that keeps on giving and will continue to give for the rest of my life on earth and my life to come in heaven.

Thank you to everyone who had anything to do with making this book a reality. My love goes out to you!

ABOUT THE AUTHOR

Borley G. Quaye is a Christ-centered social entrepreneur based in Atlanta who wears many hats. After her matriculation through Spelman College as a Psychology Major, she went on to complete a microbiology research program at the University of Pittsburgh Medical School. Borley learned fundamental skills in professionalism, work ethic and networking. From her experiences acquired from her time at Spelman and U Pitt, she decided to change her career path and follow her passions in women empowerment, business, and philanthropy. She used those skills to write her first book, Worth the Wahala, start a business, Afoko Adventures, and aid in operation of her family non-profit, The Quaye Nungua Foundation.

Her love for her Ghanaian culture inspired her to encourage young adults to travel abroad. Quaye hosts travel experiences around the world and specializes in trips to Ghana, West Africa with her tour company, Afoko Adventures. Their tours spread cultural awareness and international engagement through education, service, culture and millennial 'in the mix' living. Check out past trips and register for future trips at IG @afokoadventures and AfokoAdventures.com.

Borley also enjoys hosting red carpets, weddings, and other events. To stay up to date on all that Borley is doing, subscribe to her popular blog, HeyBorley.com. During her off time she enjoys working out, eating healthy, learning new skills, practicing photography (@bgqphoto) and decorating her new home.

REFERENCES

Notes

Chapter 5
Moss, J. "We Must Praise". The J Moss Project. GospoCentric Records, 2004.
Lewis, M. (2012, September 5). Barack Obama to Michael Lewis on a Presidential
Loss of Freedom: "You Don't Get Used to it- At least, I don't." Retrieved from http://www.vanityfair.com/news/2012/09/barack-obama-michael-lewis
Kondō, M., & Hirano, C. (2014). The life-changing magic of tidying up: The Japanese
art of decluttering and organizing (First American edition.). Berkeley: Ten Speed Press.

Chapter 6
Ramsey, D., & Ramsey, S. (2003). Financial peace revisited. New York: Viking.
Wilkinson, Bruce. (2000) The prayer of Jabez :breaking through to the blessed
life. Waterville: Thorndike Press.
Warren, R. (2002). The purpose-driven life: What on earth am I here for?.
Grand Rapids: Zondervan.
Tribbett, T. "If He did it Before (Same God)". Greater Than. Motown Gospel,
2013.

Chapter 8
National marriage and divorce rate trends for 2000-2015. Centers for
Disease Control and Prevention. Retrieved from

https://www.cdc.gov/nchs/data/dvs/national_marriage_di-vorce_rates_00-15.pdf

Chapter 10
Smith, S. "Stay with Me". In the Lonely Hour. Capitol, 2014.

Chapter 11
Life expectancy at birth, total (years). Retrieved from
    http://data.worldbank.org/indicator/SP.DYN.LE00.IN

Bible Translations

AMP
The Amplified Bible
Grand Rapids: Zondervan (1965)

NLT
New Living Translation
Wheaton, IL: Tyndale House Publishers (1996)

NIV
New International Version
Colorado Springs: International Bible Society (1978,1984)

MSG
The Message
Colorado Springs: Navpress (1993)

KJV
King James Version
New York: American Bible Society (1999)
NASB

New American Standard Bible
Anaheim, CA: Foundation Press (1973)

ESV
English Standard Version
Wheaton, IL: Crossway Bibles (2007)

Notes

_____

_____

_____

_____

_____

_____

_____

_____

_____

_____

_____

_____

_____

_____

_____

84266629R00059

Made in the USA
Columbia, SC
27 December 2017